The Soapbox Bible

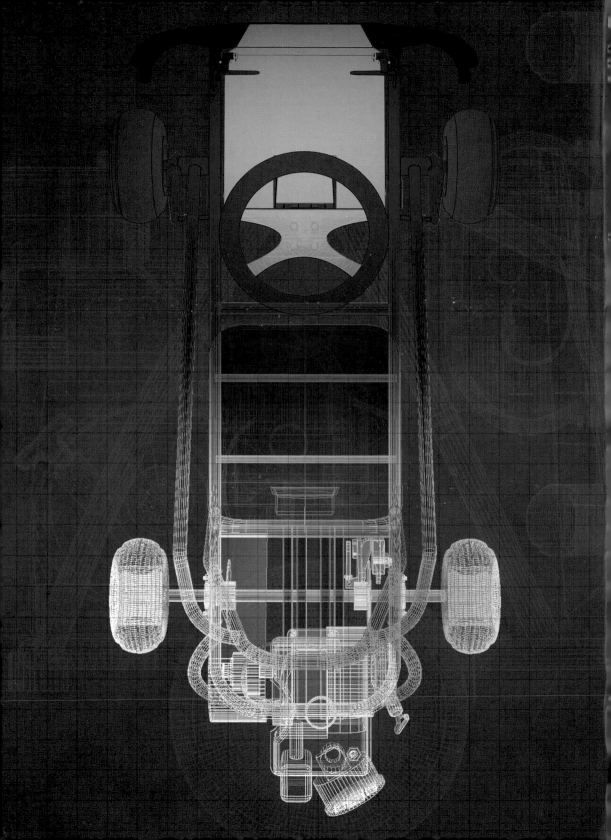

The Soapbox Bible

How to Build Your Own Soapbox, Buggy, or Go-Cart

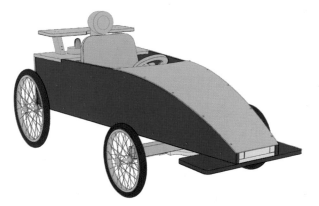

**JULIAN BRIDGEWATER
& GLYN BRIDGEWATER**

STERLING

New York / London
www.sterlingpublishing.com

Cart design and building by **Julian Bridgewater** and **Glyn Bridgewater**

Layout, illustration, and photography by **AG&G Books**

Photographs on pages 14, 15, 37, 153 by **iStockphoto**
Photograph on page 43 by **Dreamstime**

Thanks to **Harvey Bridgewater**, **Harley Bridgewater**, **Atalü Ward**,
Jessica Bridgewater, **Joseph Bridgewater**, **Reece Bulger**, **Kai Bulger,**
and **Nina Bennet-White** for testing the carts.

Library of Congress Cataloging-in-Publication Data available

2 4 6 8 10 9 7 5 3 1

Published by Sterling Publishing Co., Inc.
387 Park Avenue South, New York, NY 10016
© 2010 by Quid Publishing
Distributed in Canada by Sterling Publishing
c/o Canadian Manda Group, 165 Dufferin Street,
Toronto, Ontario, Canada M6K 3H6

Manufactured in China

Sterling ISBN 978-1-4027-6682-4

For information about custom editions, special sales, premium and
corporate purchases, please contact Sterling Special Sales
Department at 800-805-5489 or specialsales@sterlingpublishing.com.

Contents

Introduction

WHO DIDN'T HAVE A GO-CART AS A KID? Great fun, wasn't it? And competitive at times. If your friends upgraded to pneumatic wheels and brakes, it was time to go hunting for superior components and ask Dad for a hand to reinvent your poor old cart. This book will inspire you to get building again and show your kids how to have real fun; building, racing, and trying not to crash out.

WHY MAKE ONE?

This is a good question when there are so many brilliant carts available to buy. Here's the answer: you cannot beat designing, inventing, building, and racing your own cart. Ego and pride come into it, of course. But if it falls to bits, don't kick it into the ditch and give up. Instead, take it home, repair, and improve it. In any case, an old cart always has reclaimable parts in it that can be used for your next project.

TECHNIQUES

The first part of this book is all about the essentials; a bit of design, building, and racing know-how if you don't already know. Have a quick look through it before starting a project; it will give you some useful tips.

Designing from scratch is challenging, so we suggest following some of the plans in this book before doing your own.

Woodworking may be a bit easier than metalworking—DIY with wood in the home being commonplace—but if you are armed with the right tools and techniques then metalworking is also achievable.

THE BOXCART BLUEPRINT

This is the first project in the book and it lays out the bare bones of the classic boxcart; namely, an old wooden box for you to sit in, a good set of wheels, and a front axle that pivots, with a rope attached allowing you to steer. Mastering this basic design will give you an understanding of what cart design and building is all about, and will develop the skills you need to tackle the more advanced projects.

THE PROJECTS

Ten more projects follow, starting off with simple designs, progressing to intermediate designs with monocoque (shell) constructions, and ending in a few more challenging "go"-carts, meaning propelled carts.

All of the designs are just for fun, but they have all been built and tested. They may not necessarily qualify for your local derby or racetrack since rules on size, weight, and mechanics vary so much; but we think the best derby is one with no rules except that you must make it yourself and have a compulsory beercan holder somewhere in the cockpit. Joking aside, the Soapbox Racer project (see right and page 82) probably would qualify for most derbys except the All-American Soap Box Derby—you must race their kit cars—but you may want to make it longer and heavier, according to the parameters set out by the event organizers. If you do want to race, check out the rules first and adapt one of these projects to suit.

The most complex cart in this book, the Gasoline Go-Cart, is a challenging yet achievable project. It packs a punch, but it won't match the speed and handling of professionally built racing models; I wouldn't recommend taking it to your local circuit!

MAKING THE CARTS

Every project in this book lists what you need, most of which will be wood and fixings from your local DIY store, but could also include salvaged bits from old bikes or stuff you can easily buy on the internet. The exploded diagrams give you an overview of the construction and identify the parts. All dimensions are given where necessary, with guidelines given for any salvaged parts. Shaped components—curves, for example—are shown in detail. The construction procedure is broken down into easy-to-follow, illustrated steps. Measurements are given in millimeters for the maximum accuracy.

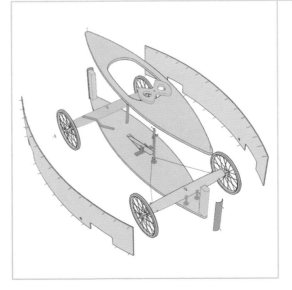

Each project has detailed diagrams like this—an exploded view of the Soapbox Racer—plus step-by-step diagrams with instructions and helpful suggestions on how you can vary your design.

1
A Brief History

The Original Boxcart

THE ORIGINAL CART WAS PROBABLY NOTHING MORE ELABORATE THAN A FEW PIECES OF WOOD LASHED TO SOME WHEELS. It's safe to assume that, wherever you are in the world, children are still building and racing carts. The materials and wheels are usually whatever is freely available, and the construction techniques often unconventional.

CARTS OF THE WORLD

In Australia, they call the basic boxcart "Billy carts" after the small square carts towed by goats and used for shifting materials or vegetables. Children would hop on the original carts—sitting on a pile of vegetables or wood—or else they would use it to go carting for the day. No doubt when the goat got fed up, the kids had to make their own cart!

In the UK the basic boxcart is called a cart, cartie, buggy, bogie, go-cart, or go-cart. The true meaning of "go" in go-cart is debatable. We maintain that it should only apply to carts that are propelled with a motor or, more usually, a gasoline engine. Others claim "go" refers to carts that have to be pushed or run downhill in order to get them moving.

In the mountains of India, kids ride on bamboo carts with bike wheels and smaller plank versions with carved wooden wheels from sections of tree trunk. In Indonesia, these carts are called "gokars."

In America, the home of the "Soapbox Derby," the origins of these stylish motorless mini racing cars lie in the soapbox cart—a cart made from a wooden packing crate and old stroller or rollerskate wheels. Of course, those were the days when you could easily find an old stroller with big wheels— these wheels are now exchanged on internet auction sites for big money!

So the go-cart, boxcart, soapbox cart, or whatever you want to call it is a handbuilt cart made from freely available materials. It usually has rope to steer and no brake.

THE SOAPBOX RACER

This vechicle is a honed, refined, and restyled version of the soapbox cart and has its roots in 1930s America. A Dayton, Ohio, newspaper reporter called Myron Scott enjoyed one such local race so much he decided to popularize it and host a nationwide event that later became known as the All-American Soap Box Derby (AASBD). Similar events take place all over the world and one basic rule applies—no motor allowed!

The AASBD holds its annual World Championship each July in Akron, Ohio. From modest beginnings the event rapidly expanded, boasting 500 racers and attracting tens of thousands of spectators by the 1950s. In its heyday, even famous Hollywood stars were turning up to enjoy the high-octane action.

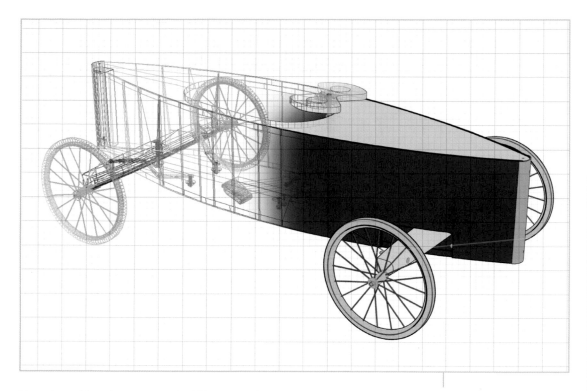

Nowadays, things have calmed down a little and event organizers have changed the rules to allow younger children to participate. Consequently, adults are now allowed to assist the younger racers in constructing their carts.

The carts themselves are high-performance vehicles, capable of reaching speeds of 35mph, and certainly a danger to anyone unlucky enough to get caught in their path. From an elevated position at the top of the track, they rely on gravity to send them flying down the hill towards the finish line.

The races are very often closely contested, with little to choose between the two soapbox racers as they cross the line. Overhead cameras have now been introduced to more accurately decide the winner of each heat.

A word of warning however: the carts in this book are not necessarily designed to be raced at speeds upwards of 30mph. They'll definitely be a lot of fun to ride, but don't be tempted to send them down a steep hill in search of the ultimate ride. You'll almost certainly lose control and in doing so run the risk of serious injury.

Three-dimensional design software allows for more detailed and accurate planning. Perfect if you want to design your own, more advanced cart.

Classic Designs

BEFORE TALENTED DESIGNERS AND EXPENSIVE CONSTRUCTION KITS BECAME COMMONPLACE, CARTS WERE THING OF UNIQUE BEAUTY. They were hastily built carts, made from whatever was to hand, and probably by an already exhausted dad. No wonder, then, that the result was usually something simple!

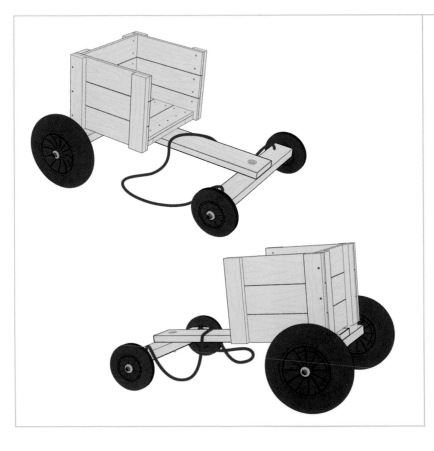

Here we have the classic boxcart, also shown from the rear. It does not get more basic than this, unless you discard the box and hang on to the plank for dear life!

BASIC BOXCART ANATOMY

Four wheels are fixed to two axles. The axle is the shaft between the wheels and is normally a metal rod that fits through the holes in the wheels. Usually the axles need reinforcing with pieces of wood. The axles are set apart in order to balance the cart. The rear axle is fixed firmly and squarely to a strong plank and the front axle is pivoted to the front end of that plank. A box is fixed at the back to keep the driver in place. The front axle is used both as a footrest and for steering. The rope provides an additional method of steering, but is also used for pulling the cart.

Here is the archetypal soapbox racer. It has the same components as the basic cart, but is designed to look more like a classic car. The steering wheel is an obvious departure; with most racers this is cable steering, which is very similar to rope steering. The cable is wound around the steering column and activates the steering. Brakes are an important addition.

LASH-UPS

When you were under pressure to produce a cart from thin air, and often with a limited toolkit, design would probably have taken a back seat to carefully considered improvisation. So pieces of wood were used as they were found. Nails of all lengths were knocked through and their ends bent over. The wheels might have seen better days and bearings may not even have been invented! Fortunately, this haphazard and dangerous construction method has given way to a more considered approach. Our chapter on the Basic Boxcart shows you how to build a simple cart that is fun to ride and safe.

STYLE

There comes a time when your trusty cart is overshadowed by some souped-up version, at which point it's time to elaborate on the basic design. This could involve improving the wheels and bearings, a fabulous paint job, a twin horn, something to flick the spokes, or a whole new body shell.

Soapbox Racing

BUILDING YOUR OWN CART AND RACING IT IS A
FINE AMBITION. There are hundreds of races to
compete in, not just the most famous of them all—
the All-American Soap Box Derby. Most races have
rules that apply to the design and build of the cart,
plus rules that apply to the race itself.

A close-up of two soapbox
derby race cars perched and
ready to go. The nose of the
car is up against a mechanical
starting device that flips out of
the way to start the race.

RULES

There are a number of rules common to most race events:
• The cart must have at least four wheels
• The cart must be motorless
• The cart must have brakes of some description, although they are rarely used!
• The driver must wear a crash helmet
• The cart must be made—or at least partly assembled—by the driver

DESIGN AND BUILD

Most races award points for build quality and creativity in design. An exception to that is the All-American Soap Box Derby, which uses standard kits and removes that part of the challenge. But this aspect of the competition does make a soapbox race more fun, more educational, and more inclusive—so look out for your local derby and start your design and engineering career. Build quality obviously refers to the standard of engineering, craftsmanship, and finish. The design part has a lot to do with originality, but is mostly about style. For style tips you can look at car styling generally, but especially sports cars, super cars, and racing cars. Think about aerodynamic shapes.

THE RACE

The course is always a downhill stretch and is often a fairly straight run, hence the limited steering ability of many soapbox racers. This, however, really does depend on the location —some courses are more complex. Braking is a bad idea unless you have to avoid a collision. Jerking the car forward is often not allowed. The winner will probably be the driver in the most aerodynamic car; in other words, one that is well-constructed, and with no wobbles and rattles. High-quality bearings and an aerodynamic body position will also be crucial. Wheels, whether solid or pneumatic, don't seem to make a great deal of difference.

Two soapbox derby racers are neck and neck as they cross the finish line.

2

Principles of Design

Reclaiming and Sourcing Materials

AH, THE AGE-OLD PROBLEM: WHERE TO FIND THE MATERIALS? Often you have no money or don't know where to start. For basic carts, here are some tips on reclaiming materials; for advanced designs, we offer some notes on where to find the more unusual components.

RECLAIMING MATERIALS

It is amazing what people throw away. Some people take lengths of unused prepared timber to the dump simply because they want their garage to look tidy! It is not uncommon to find a discarded bike with perfectly good wheels that can be reclaimed and reused. The same goes for garden play equipment and old strollers. Call it being thrifty, call it scrounging, but reclaiming materials helps the environment and saves you money.

WHERE TO LOOK

Obviously any old bike, stroller, and timber around your own house is ideal. After that, try your neighbors, family, and friends. After that you can look out for wheels at your local dump, although some dumps do not allow items that include wheels to be reclaimed or sold for reasons of "safety and insurance," regardless of the environmental impact. Boot sales and yard sales are brilliant places to find wheels and wood. The Freecycle Network (often abbreviated to TFN or just known as Freecycle) is one of the best places of all.

TIMBER

Like all materials, timber is expensive and especially so when you only need a few bits for a cart. Your local DIY superstore is obviously the convenient place to find seasoned, machined bits of wood, but it is also the most expensive place to go. A sawmill is not the best place as the wood will be unseasoned —that's okay for a rough cart but no good for anything else. Timber yards, on the other hand, will often have a heap of offcuts from seasoned wood that you can root through and find some gems for next to nothing. Builders' and carpenters' offcuts are brilliant too, so it's always wise to

BUYING ON THE INTERNET

The miracle of internet auction websites has transformed the go-cart enthusiast's world enormously. No more wandering around fairs in the vain hope of finding the right wheel or sprocket. Now you can find every part imaginable, and some more. Secondhand parts or part-finished go-cart projects are a good way to go. If you are aiming to race gasoline-engine go-carts, then all the necessary components and accessories are available via mail order.

make friends with a local builder. We do not recommend salvaging wood from a dump or a skip unless you have permission to do so and have assurance that the wood is not contaminated, which may not always be obvious. Lead paint and some treated woods are hazardous and should be avoided.

Solid wood should be free from knots, but that is not so easy to find nowadays, and probably impossible if you are buying from a DIY store. In that case you should check that the knots are not so large that the piece of wood would snap too easily. Timber for soapbox racers—those entered for a race—should be acquired from a specialist timber yard that can supply machined wood of the highest quality.

Plywood quality varies greatly, as does its price. The plywood in your local DIY store is poor- to medium-quality, but will suffice for most jobs. It will not give a smooth surface for painting, unless you sand and fill for a very long time. For top results, you should buy birch plywood from a specialist timber supplier. However, with careful selection you will be able to avoid buying the ultra-expensive A-grade plywood.

METAL

DIY stores now often have a large stand full of a wide range of metal sections, threaded rod, aluminum trim, steel, stainless steel, and aluminum sheet. This is a great starting point since you are unlikely to need much for your cart—unless it is a motor-driven car, of course.

You can salvage metal tube easily, as already mentioned, but it is fairly cheap to buy anyway from a metal supplier. Typically, however, they are unhelpful when you need only a small amount, so put on your best smile.

PARTS

Solid racing wheels are almost impossible to buy new—apart from AASBD wheels if you want those—but secondhand ones can occasionally be found on the internet.

New bike wheels are easy to buy but very expensive, as are new wheelbarrow and sackbarrow wheels. Secondhand bike and stroller wheels are the best option.

Go-cart (powered cart) parts are readily available on the internet.

BUYING KITS AND PLANS

There are some really great kits to buy. The All-American Soap Box Derby kits are fantastic but obviously intended for that event. There are also cart enthusiasts out there who supply high-quality kits for basic boxcarts, soapbox racers, pedal carts, motorized carts, and gasoline-engine carts (see page 155) . You can also buy cart plans with advice on where to buy parts. Plans are not always that great, so try to get ones with testimonials or reviews.

Design

GET THE BASICS RIGHT AND THEN WORRY ABOUT
STYLING. Dimensions are sometimes critical.
Perhaps they are not so important in a basic cart, but
more complicated carts certainly need planning
from the start to ensure they are at least functional.
Once the fundamentals are in place, you can begin to
look at styling your cart.

DIMENSIONS

You can work out
dimensions by looking
at the plans in this book
or by mocking up an
idea quickly and testing
it. This can be no more
complicated than sitting
on a chair, extending
your legs, and measuring
the distance between
your feet and the back
of the chair. The various
designs in this book are
suitable for different
ages. The blueprint
cart is even suitable
for adults. If you are
making a cart for a child,
take measurements
first, before beginning
construction.

Ergonomics, or how
our bodies interact with
objects, are a factor.
Again, you can mock
this up by sitting in a
chair and working out
where to put the steering
rope or wheel, pedals,
handlebars, and so on.

DRAWING

Many people groan at
the thought of having
to draw anything, but
all you are doing is
making visual notes to
help you understand
the options available to
you. Drawing can be a
way of working out the
structure. For example,
does it look strong
enough, or can you see
some weak points?
Does it need additional
reinforcement? What will
be the best method of
construction? Drawing
is also used for plotting
out the shapes, either
to a scale or more likely
full-size. Automotive
designers draw large
elevations—front view,
side view, and plan view,
for example—often
at half-size, but also
full-size. You can do
the same on a piece of
hardboard, which would
usually be painted white.

INSPIRATION

Cars are the most obvious starting point, especially racing cars. A trip to a motor museum is also a great
idea. Serious competitors are not so likely to show their carts to you in any detail, so if you are lucky enough
to live near a museum that has fine examples of soapbox racers then so much the better. If your cart has a
theme then research that—for example, old Mercedes or Formula 1 cars. If you are short of ideas, look at
cart races on the internet; Flickr and YouTube have hundreds of examples.

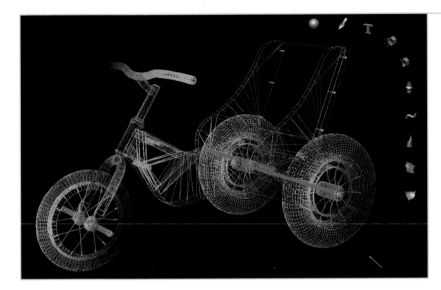

Three-dimensional design programs can be useful for working out dimensions and angles before you start building. This is the Amapi program, but there are many other alternatives including Google's free software, SketchUp.

This method is a great way of refining your shapes as well. Look at any car and you will probably appreciate the dynamic curves and overall shape that the designers have come up with. Those shapes are all deliberately arranged to give the car a particular feel —sporty, rugged, sleek, practical, friendly, quirky, etc. If you are designing a soapbox racer, for example, not only do you want an aerodynamic shape, you also want it to look great and be appreciated by the judges. So when you are ready to refine the body shape, decide how you want it to look. A quirky look is quite easy to pull off, of course—this often happens by accident as well—but something sleek, classy, maybe a bit retro, is more challenging.

COPYING PLANS

This is a good idea at first, particularly if you find design difficult or boring.

SHAPES

It seems obvious to say, but curves and rounded corners are good ideas. Curved shapes are more aerodynamic and rounded corners are safer. Straight lines and square shapes also look a bit dull in this context. When you plan curves you need to either use a radius—part of a circle—or a smooth curve. Hand-drawn curves can look lumpy, so always use smooth curves plotted using a long, thin, flexible edge. In this book we have suggested you ask a friend to hold and bend a sheet of flexible plywood to a suitable curve that you can draw around.

SKETCHING

Sketching is a good habit to get into, especially if you want to develop designs with a high degree of interest and originality. Recording good ideas in a sketchbook will help you focus your ideas. By sketching them you can rapidly work through and dismiss bad or boring ideas, allowing you to focus on the promising ones. Annotate your sketches—especially if they are a bit rough—so you don't forget later on. If you are not so good on the engineering side, you can show your sketches to someone who is, for some advice.

Techniques

MAKING CARTS IS EASY, ESPECIALLY IF YOU ALREADY HAVE SOME DIY EXPERIENCE. For most designs you need little woodworking experience, so don't be afraid to jump right in. You are likely to need power tools, so for safety's sake and for the best results you must follow the manufacturer's instructions.

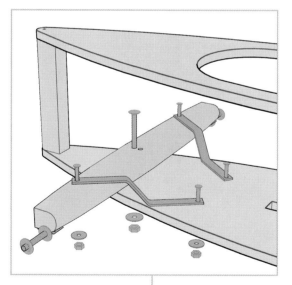

As with most DIY projects, if you break it down into small procedures it becomes much easier. The detailed diagrams in this book, like the one above, guide you through every step.

WOODWORKING

You could probably do all the woodworking in this book with not much more than a jigsaw, a cordless drill/driver with bits—drill bits for various size holes and driver bits for fixing screws—plus a hammer for knocking in pins and small nails. So that's good news if you have no tools and have to go out and buy some. The most inexpensive will be fine. Follow the instructions in the tool manual's and you will do just fine.

If, however, you are a DIY whiz then you are sure to have a workbench of some kind, maybe a planer, maybe a compound miter saw, and so on. The more the merrier; these tools are obviously going to give you an advantage and enable you to build the design accurately and neatly—not so many splinters, in other words!

Judges love to see well-finished carts; here are some tips.

• Straight edges: ensure these are straight and correct by planing

• Curves: these should be smooth. Again, you can plane these smooth, if it's an outward (external) curve, or use a compass plane for internal curves. Routing is also an option. For example, you can make a perfectly curved template in thin

DESIGN NOTES FOR WOOD

Wood is particularly easy to work with and the most versatile of all construction materials. It has some unique qualities from a structural point of view: it is very stiff and strong in compression and tension, relative to its weight. It can be bent to follow curves—for example, steambent, laminated, or just flexible enough to bend—and carved into smooth shapes. It is easy to cut and drill as well. Added to that you have its appearance; wood color and grain is beautiful and adds a "classic" feel to any design.

hardboard and copy that to much thicker plywood using a router and a straight cutter with a bearing attached

- Fixings: these should be neatly countersunk with a good-quality countersink bit or else plugged over with matching wood using counter-bore and matching plug-cutting

bits. Pins should be knocked below the surface and filled or not used at all. Modern glues and clamping techniques negate the need for pins

METALWORKING

Most of the projects require some cutting and drilling, which is simple enough with a hacksaw and sharp, high-speed steel drill bits. ALWAYS file off sharp burrs and round over edges immediately. Do not leave it until you slice yourself, or someone else for that matter. Using stainless steel can save you a lot of time as no paint is required, and it looks great. The same goes for aluminum sheet or trim. Aluminum sheet is easy to cut with a jigsaw fitted with a metal-cutting blade.

Welding is not explained in this book as we recommend taking lessons from an expert or asking a fabricator to do the work for you. You can sometimes avoid welding by using bolts, but the results are rarely as satisfactory.

DESIGN NOTES FOR METAL

Metal is, of course, very strong, especially at the joints. If these joints are pivot joints, bolted, riveted, or welded then you probably have an incredibly strong structure. However, metal is considered—by woodworkers at least—to be tougher to work with. There is also the problem of weight. Metal is very dense, so even small pieces are heavy. That is why you need to use tubular steel or create stiffness in the structure using ribs. These can be fashioned into boxlike structures—sometimes called *monocoque* structures—as in the modern car.

SAFETY

When you are cutting and sanding wood, wear a dust mask to avoid breathing in the dust. Eye protection, such as goggles or a face shield, is recommended for all power tool use. Support and clamp your work down so it does not move about or fall down and cause an accident. Never put your hands near a blade, cutter, or drill, and always follow the manufacturer's instructions. Circular saws, grinders, and welding gear are particularly dangerous, so you should always treat them with respect.

Soapbox Control

WHEN IT COMES TO DRIVING OR RACING, IT
OBVIOUSLY HELPS TO BE IN CONTROL OF YOUR
CART. Here are some tips that may speed you along
or save you from becoming the next soapbox racing
casualty. There are some important factors to take
note of that will help avoid unnecessary accidents.

COURSE
No matter what cart you
have, you need to look at
the field, track, beach,
private road, or whatever
course you aim to take,
and ask yourself: is it
safe to go that way? In a
cart you have only limited
control. In the basic cart
you have no brakes and
limited steering, so it
is not difficult to lose
control going down a
steep hill. Many people
can remember carting

Cart steering is usually
limited and nowhere near as
good as car steering. Here
is a typical soapbox steering
example using cable wrapped
around the column. The front
axle pivots as you turn the
steering wheel. It is designed
for relatively straight courses;
therefore, the axle does not
pivot more than an inch or two
either way.

SAFETY

We have compiled detailed safety notes on pages 150–3, but it is important to reiterate the importance
of careful preparation. If you are going to race then you must wear a helmet, even if you are just playing
around. A cycle helmet will do the job just fine. Don't go carting anywhere without having checked the
location first. In many cases it is illegal to use a cart for reasons of safety. Keep your hands away from
wheels, chains, motors, brakes, pivot points, and all other moving parts.

CAMBER

Adverse camber refers to sections of a road that slope in the opposite direction to its curve, making it difficult to stay tight to the inside of the curve. Camber also applies to the wheels on motorized carts. The best steering and suspension on production models will tilt the wheels inward slightly at the top. This will improve the grip of the tires on corners and is called negative camber.

as a kid and one of their friends crashing out in a big way. We know someone who knocked out quite a few perfectly good teeth after a go-cart stunt went wrong. There are also the dangers to other people to consider. If somebody appears unexpectedly, you have to take evasive action. If you are out of control then this won't be possible.

Resist the temptation to launch yourself off the top of a huge hill and don't let anyone do it in your cart either!

Naturally, in a race you do not need to worry about the safety of the course—that is taken care of—but you do need to master control of your cart.

Your body position in a soapbox racer is important and can help you go faster. A reclined or forward-facing position is more aerodynamic than an

upright position and your position in relation to the wheel base, or area inside the wheels, and the distribution of weight over the cart has a great effect on your control of the cart when cornering.

Weight distribution is also very important with motorized go-cart racing, so you will often see carts with a very low center of gravity. Often the driver will be positioned alongside the engine in a central position.

For maximum stability, four wheels are essential. They should be spaced equally, marking out a rectangle.

For maximum control when cornering at speed, the steering should follow the Ackermann principle (see page 116). This angles each of the front wheels slightly differently so that they align with the radius of a curve in the track. This is not the case in basic carts or even soapbox racers, which more often specifically ban

"mechanical steering," as it is sometimes referred to. These considerations are less important if the track you are racing is predominantly straight.

All brakes, except disk brakes and drum brakes, are fairly inadequate in relation to the weight and momentum of the cart (see page 38). It is therefore doubly important that you choose a site that is as free from potential obstacles as possible.

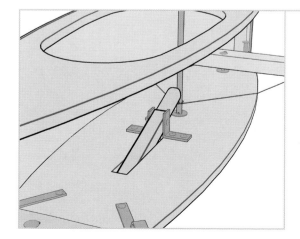

This shows a soapbox racer brake lever that is pulled upward and presses a brake pad directly on the ground. This, or a vertical plunger variation of it, is the typical method of braking. Careful though: pull too hard and it will shift the direction your cart is headed!

3

The Boxcart Blueprint

The Basic Boxcart

THIS IS PRETTY MUCH THE SIMPLEST BOXCART RACER IMAGINABLE, BUT IT WILL WORK JUST FINE AND TEACH YOU A LOT ABOUT CONSTRUCTION. Boxcarts can be made from old reclaimed bits; a packing crate for the seat and a good set of wheels are the first things to look out for. If you can't get your hands on these, then head down to your local DIY store.

YOU WILL NEED

Some basic tools:
- Hammer
- Screwdriver
- File
- Coarse sandpaper
- Saw
- Tape measure
- Pencil
- T-square
- Drill and drill bits
- Clamp
- Wrench
- Hacksaw
- Pliers

If you have all of the above then you probably also have a portable workbench, which is ideal. Or else, you will need to find a suitable place to support your materials while you work.

Some wood:
- If you can find a wooden packing crate then fine; if not, you can make a seat using pieces reclaimed from a discarded pallet
- Check that it is not a returnable pallet
- The other pieces of wood are easy to buy from your local DIY store, or you may even have an old bit knocking about. Think of any broken or discarded furniture you may have in the garage, but make sure it's not an antique first!
- Check that the sections are strong and avoid knots at weak points in the structure

Some metal:
- Axles can be tubular or solid, but you need to think about strength. A 12 mm (½ in) tubular axle might be strong enough, but will it last?
- Solid axles are generally better. Most DIY stores will have these, or you can go to a metal supplier
- Axle brackets can be right-angle brackets bent and reshaped a bit, and the split pins can be lengths of coathanger wire folded in half
- All the other nuts, bolts, washers, and screws are easy to find

You also need:
- Four wheels and some rope for steering and pulling

The completed boxcart. This is a no-frills version, but the construction process is fast and simple, making this the quickest and cheapest way to get yourself mobile. All you need now, of course, is a hill to run it down . . .

600 mm (23 ½ in)

800 mm (31 ½ in)

600 mm (23 ½ in)

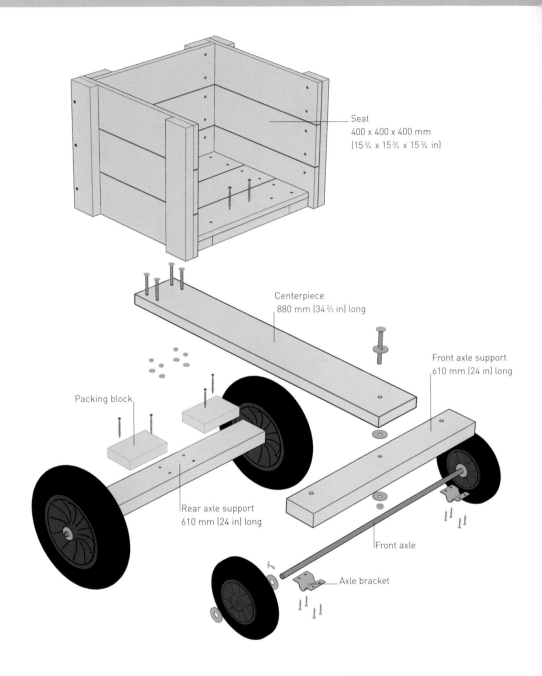

Seat
400 x 400 x 400 mm
(15 ¾ x 15 ¾ x 15 ¾ in)

Centerpiece
880 mm (34 ⅔ in) long

Front axle support
610 mm (24 in) long

Packing block

Rear axle support
610 mm (24 in) long

Front axle

Axle bracket

An exploded view identifying
the components and showing
how they are assembled.

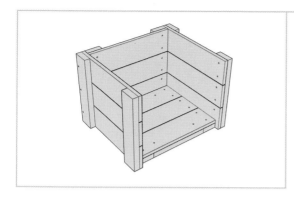

01 Start by carefully removing the lid and one side of the packing case so you've got a box with sides and a back, which you can sit in. You may need to reinforce the box using screws. Check that there are no ends of nails or screws sticking out—if there are, file them off. Use coarse sandpaper to remove any splinters and sharp corners that may cause injury. Put this to one side.

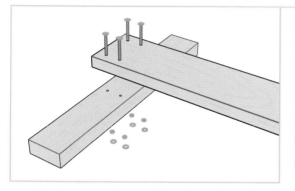

02 Cut the centerpiece and axle supports to length. Now sort out how the rear axle support is joined to the centerpiece. If you want to be accurate, use a tape measure, pencil, and T-square to mark where the pieces go. Mark where you want the holes on the centerpiece and drill them. To minimize splinters on the underside, first place a piece of scrap wood underneath the piece to be drilled. Position the centerpiece over the back crosspiece and clamp them together. Now drill through both thicknesses to get perfectly aligned holes. While still clamped, put in the bolts, add the washers and nuts, and do them up tightly.

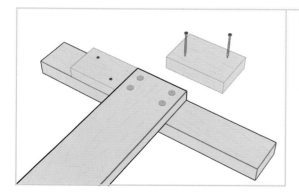

03 Add the two packing blocks. These are just bits of wood the same thickness as the centerpiece. They stop the seat from rocking from side to side. You may want to put the seat in position and mark how far it extends either side. This can be a guide to how big the packing blocks need to be.

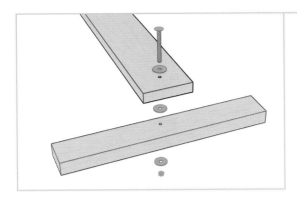

04 Next you need to bolt the front end of the centerpiece to the front crosspiece using a chunky bolt (kingpin) and large washers. It is these washers that allow the bits to pivot and give a smooth steering action. Again, if you want to be accurate, use a tape measure to mark the hole positions—there is no need to overlap and drill through pieces this time. Note how the axle in the diagram for step 05 is placed centrally and the kingpin exits to one side. If you don't want to do this you can use a shorter bolt and recess the nut and washer so the axle can pass over the top.

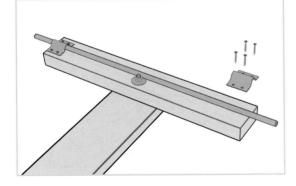

05 Work out the lengths of your axles. This will depend on your wheels. You need to allow enough to take the wheels and washers and leave a stub (12 mm or so) sticking out either side to take the split pins. Cut the axles to length and drill holes for the split pins. We are showing how to fix the front axle, but the procedure is the same for the rear. Turn your structure upside down, mark a center line on the crosspiece, position the axle with equal amounts sticking out from either end, and use the axle brackets and screws to fix it to the wood. The axle is not supposed to turn—the wheels spin on the axle.

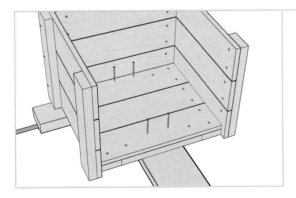

06 Place the seat centrally and squarely on the structure. Check the position with a tape measure, mark with a pencil, and fix the seat to the centerpiece with four or more substantial screws. The positioning of these screws will depend on your crate construction, but choose positions where the wood is thickest.

BRAKES

Basic carts don't use—or really need—brakes at all. There is usually room within the design for the driver to drag his or her feet along the ground in such a fashion that reduces the speed of the cart; either that or steer it back up an incline until it slows down. There are, however, simple brake mechanisms that you can build yourself out of easy-to-obtain components. Old-fashioned door hinges work surprisingly well, as does half a sneaker.

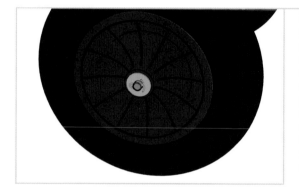

07 Fit the wheels. Put large washers on the ends of the axles first and then push on the wheel. If you cannot find wheels with holes in to match your axle then you may want to improve the fit by using a section of steel tube slid over the axle. Another problem you may have is the sides of the wheel rubbing up against the sides of the cart. Use more washers or a piece of tube slid over the axle if you need more of a gap. More washers follow the wheels and then push the split pins through the holes in the axles and bend over the ends to secure the wheels. If the wheels are a bit wobbly, try adding more washers for a tighter fit.

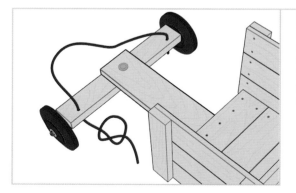

08 Drill holes near the ends of the front crosspiece to take the steering/pulling rope. Tie a knot near one end and thread through one hole from the underside. Thread the other end downward through the other hole. Check for length, tie a knot in the other end, and cut off the excess. That's it, you're done!

4

Customize Your Boxcart

Seats and Bars

CART IN COMFORT AND STYLE WITH THESE
SIMPLE ADDITIONS. One step up from an old crate
is a comfortable seat; there are a few easy options to
consider, including reusing old plastic seats. Bars,
whether bull bars, roll bars, or a complete cage, can
also be made using reclaimed materials.

SUITABLE SEATS

Strong polypropylene seats like the ones on school chairs are great and should be relatively easy to find.
Failing that, any old back and seat that can be separated from the frame are also okay. You obviously need
to check you are using a mass-produced worthless chair and not destroying an antique!

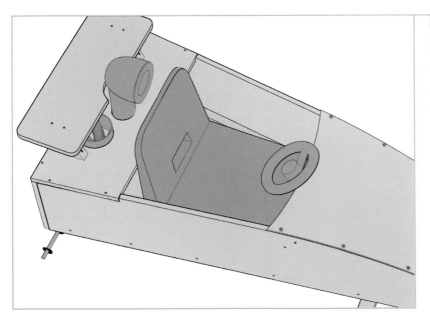

Plastic seats like the one here
are usually available in five
sizes, so choose one that fits.
Detach the metal frame, and
bolt or screw the seat to the
cart. The original fixing points
or lugs can be used if they
occur in convenient positions.

As well as providing additional protection to the driver, roll bars will lend your cart a rugged, "all-terrain" look.

SEATS

As well as plastic chairs you can also use baby or toddler car seats. By the time you have stripped out the polystyrene padding you have a seat easily big enough for a much older child, plus it has seat belts—ideal! Old carts often made use of worn-out woven chairs like wicker or Lloyd Loom (woven wire wrapped in paper) as they were easy to come by and very comfortable.

Or, why not borrow a cushion for your horrible hard crate?

BARS

Bars give your cart a rugged, sporty look. Look at dune buggies, jeeps, and off-road racing carts for inspiration. Just about any shapes can be used, but bear in mind the functional aspect of the bars; they are there to protect you from impact or rolling over, so they need to form a protective barrier around you and be a strong structure. To this end you will often see triangulation used in a design. For serious carting, you need custom-built bars, but just for jazzing up your boxcart you can use pieces of bent tubing or frames reclaimed from chairs or old play equipment. Obviously you have to take great care to join and finish the bars so you eliminate any sharp edges and spiky fixings. Neglecting to do that can lead to some nasty cuts. Pad bars with foam tubes like the ones plumbers use to insulate pipes. Add bungee-style cargo nets—nets on the back or sides suspended from the bars to give extra protection—or solar-powered searchlights.

Brakes

BRAKES ARE NOT NEEDED ON BASIC CARTS, BUT
ARE AN OBVIOUS ADVANTAGE. With brakes you can
push the performance of your cart just that little bit
further and still maintain control. Here we discuss
the easiest options first and then touch on the
sophisticated types for more advanced designs.

BRAKE LEVER

This is an easy addition
to make and very
effective, but does have
the disadvantage of
affecting your steering.
It brakes one wheel
only, so you will need
to pull the steering
around to compensate.
All you need is a piece of
wood—it can be shaped
to make a comfortable
handle like the one
shown here—pivoted to
the side of your cart with
a thick rubber pad fixed
to the end. Thick rubber
pads are difficult to get,
so you can use a piece
of old tire or old sneaker
sole instead.

Arrange the wood
and pivot point so the
leverage works to your
advantage and yet does
not obstruct the wheel in

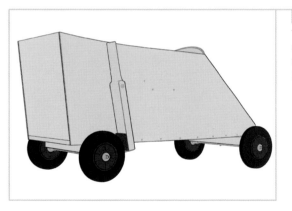

The simplest of all brakes is
a lever attached to the side of
the cart that presses a rubber
pad on the wheel.

normal use. This method
works for basic boxcarts
and for soapbox racers
like the one above. Could
two be used? Probably,
if you have hands-free
foot-controlled steering.

BRAKE PLUNGER

This is like a handbrake
on a car—usually
situated somewhere
central inside the cockpit
of a soapbox racer—and
not normally found on
basic carts, although
it can easily be applied
to those. The brake is a
wooden lever, pivoted in
the floor of the cart and

held off the ground by a
spring. When the lever
is pulled it presses a
rubber pad against the
ground. It sounds rough
and it is!

BIKE BRAKE TYPES

Bike brakes have evolved over the years from the first spoon brakes, whereby a pad pressed onto the wheel, to rod-actuated brakes and modern caliper and cantilever brakes, which all squeeze blocks of rubber on the wheel rim. All of these types are suitable for reusing on carts that use bike wheels. Modern bike disk brakes (with a disk on the hub) or drum brakes can also be used, but back-pedal brakes (coaster brakes) will not be useful unless you are building a pedal cart.

BIKE BRAKES

What could be easier than using bike brakes, you might ask? If you are using bike wheels then they are a logical option but also challenging to get right. They are incredibly effective, and this can be one of the problems. They clamp so tightly to the wheel rim that with too much weight and momentum they are likely to rip off the cart unless you fix them with a very strong bracket. Make the bracket from bent or welded steel strap and engineer it so that it overhangs the wheels but remains firmly braced against the cart. Use bolts to fix it, as screws will not hold. Use on one or both back wheels or both of the front wheels. Steering is affected with unequal braking so these need to be balanced. Run brakes into the same brake lever, using the cable and lever that were on the bike.

DISK BRAKES

Bike disk brakes can be used and are a wonderful—and very effective—addition to the cart. Disk brakes of the kind shown below are a better option for motorized carts, although drum brakes are also used in some cases.

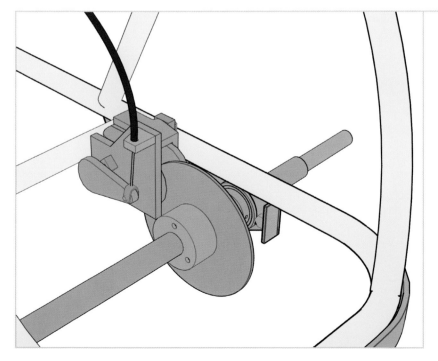

Disk brakes can be reclaimed from existing motorized vehicles or bought specifically for the job. The disks are prone to rusting, bashing, cracking, and warping, but can easily be replaced.

Advanced Steering

ROPE STEERING IS SIMPLE AND EFFECTIVE,
BUT IT IS NOT THE ONLY WAY TO CONTROL YOUR
CART. Here we show the alternative methods most
commonly used for carts. As for reengineering
your basic boxcart, it's best to try bent-rod or cable
steering first. The Ackermann type is reserved for
carts with split axles and is more complicated.

BENT-ROD STEERING

This is the type of steering you commonly find on toy carts. The steering wheel turns a rod that has a crook or hook at the bottom end. The crook is passed through slots in a plate which is attached to, but set at a distance from, the front straight axle. The plate and axle are pivoted to the underside of the cart. The end of the crook moves the plate side-to-side, pivoting the axle. It is a little tricky to get right—to give maximum rotation and least slack or obstruction—so the carts in this book that use this type of steering include templates with critical dimensions for the slots and pivot point.

CABLE STEERING

This is surprisingly simple but also effective. However, the steering extent is usually limited and therefore not normally used on carts that need a small steering circle—turning in your back yard, for example. It is best suited for use in soapbox racers that only need limited steering capability—basically just enough to keep the cart on the road. It also is slower acting; you can turn the steering wheel around more than once, as in a car with rack-and-pinion steering. The steering works by winding a cable around the steering column. As the column is rotated the cable shortens one side and lengthens the other. The ends of the cable pivot a straight axle.

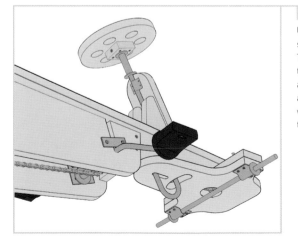

Underside detail of a cart showing bent-rod steering. The steering column needs to be supported at the approximate angle shown or at an angle closer to 90°. It won't work at 45° or less as the rod will jam.

RACK-AND-PINION STEERING

This is the most effective steering option and, although it is suitable for carts, it is usually used only on custom-built models. It is the kind used in cars. The circular pinion on the steering column engages teeth on the rack, thereby creating sideways movement. The sideways movement is used to move the steering linkage in the same or similar way as shown below in the Ackermann mechanism. DIY cart-builders can reuse the rack and pinion from a small scrapped car—this will be a great project if you like a challenge!

ACKERMANN STEERING

This is an invention—a geometric arrangement of steering linkage—that is used in most cars. The front split axles (independent axle stubs) are pivoted from the chassis, arms extend from each stub, and are linked to each other with a rod to form a parallelogram—almost. Almost, because it is deliberately adjusted so it is not a perfect parallelogram. That is the whole point of Ackermann steering; it rotates the wheels in unison but to varying degrees. In Ackermann steering (when the wheels are set straight), a straight line drawn through the pivot points in the linkage (A and B in the diagram at right) should pass through the centerpoint of the back axle. This arrangement ensures the wheels on the outside and inside of a turn trace out circles of different radii.

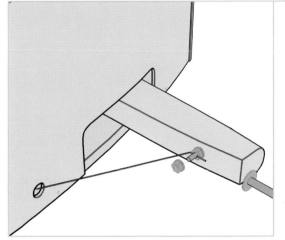

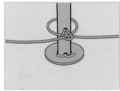

Detail of cable steering on a soapbox racer. The cable is tensioned at the end of the axle and wrapped several times around the steering column, as indicated below (see also page 82).

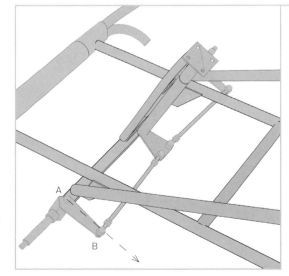

Steering geometry for a motorized cart that can be adjusted using the rods. This shows steering using arms set squarely to the axle stubs, which is easy to make when you are unsure of the precise cart dimensions, although not ideal. To refine this, follow the Ackermann steering geometry described in this section.

Paint, Graphics, and Accessories

A GOOD PAINT JOB AND SOME FINISHING TOUCHES WILL GIVE YOU AN ADVANTAGE OVER OTHER RACERS. Good design and engineering makes the fastest cart for sure, but for extra points try some of these techniques and ideas to improve the appearance of your cart.

PREPARATION

It's all in the preparation —boring perhaps, but true. If you start off with good-quality plywood you can reduce the amount of work needed to get the surface smooth. Otherwise there is probably some filling, sanding, and priming to do. For wood, start by sanding with medium sandpaper and finish with fine. Fill holes if necessary. Paint the bare wood with a primer. When dry, lightly sand with super-fine sandpaper.

Metal should be filed or ground smooth around welded joints and primed with metal primer.

PAINTING

On wood, after sanding the primed surface, you can apply your paint. Allow to dry and again sand very lightly with super-fine sandpaper to remove "nibs" (roughness caused by dust or raised grain). Apply a final coat. Good-quality synthetic brushes minimize brushmarks.

On metal, after the primer is dry, you can apply the color. Several coats are required.

Spray paint can be used on wood and metal and gives the best finish, but requires several coats and is very wasteful of paint. Use spray cans, an electric spray kit, or a spraygun with a compressor. You must work in a ventilated area and wear a breathing mask to protect yourself from the paint.

MASKING

If you are a skilled artist then you can paint wonderful things on your cart and wow the judges, but otherwise you may need a little help in the form of masking or stencils. If you need a circle, for example, you can cut out a circular hole in thick paper, temporarily fix it to the cart with sprayed repositional glue, and spray over it. Allow to dry and remove the stencil.

For stripes, use masking tape and paper to cover the areas you wish to remain unpainted. Paint and remove as before.

For lettering, ask a skilled artist to do it for you by hand, try it yourself, or ask a signage workshop to make some vinyl lettering for you to stick on. You need a super-smooth surface for the best results.

ACCESSORIES

Kids customize their bikes with stickers (decals), clickers (something to flick the spokes), tassels, and flags; some people change their wheels for alloys and graft on air intakes and spoilers. You can add these same features to your cart. Cool colors and trim will complete the transformation.

ACCESSORIES

- Safety flags
- Grip tape (checkered anti-slip tape)
- Water bottle
- Grab handles
- Seat belts
- Reflectors
- Horn
- Seat cover
- Outdoor cover to keep your cart dry
- Stickers (decals)
- Competition mesh
- Spoilers
- Twin exhaust pipes
- Aluminum trim

Custom paint the quick way. Convincing flames sprayed over a black background can be created using a simple flame-shaped stencil.

5
Advanced Designs

The Off-Road Cart

THIS CART GIVES YOU THE EXTRA STYLE AND TRACTION NEEDED FOR ALL-TERRAIN DRIVING. The dune buggy appearance is more than just styling; the deep-tread wheels give you a better chance in the rough, and if the going gets tough and you lose control the padded roll cage will offer some protection.

YOU WILL NEED

Some basic tools:
- Tape measure
- Pencil
- Saw
- Drill/driver with bits
- Hacksaw
- File
- Pliers
- Coarse sandpaper
- A bench with a vise is a definite advantage

Some wood:
- You need a piece of thick plywood for the base
- A couple of small section sticks for reinforcing the sides

- Some chunky wood for the axle supports
- The axle supports should be free from massive knots that will cause a weakness
- The plywood could be discarded from a building site
- The bits of wood can be short lengths that you might easily find in a heap of offcuts

Some metal:
- 12 mm (½ in) diameter solid axles are ideal; most DIY stores will have these. Lighter sections are likely to bend when you really go off-road
- Axle brackets
- Split pins
- Nuts
- Bolts
- Washers
- Screws—similar to those in the blueprint project—are needed

For the roll cage we salvaged a chair frame and pieces of tube from a swing. If you can't find these, ask a metalworker to bend and weld a suitable frame.

You also need:
- An old baby car seat; when you take all the padding off you will have a large rugged seat shell with seat belts
- Look out for a tough set of wheels, preferably knobbly ones
- Some rope for steering and pulling

This cart must be ruggedly built to survive rough terrain. It's fun to ride, but do keep in mind it's not your average all-terrain vehicle (ATV); this cut-down version is devoid of suspension and shock absorbers.

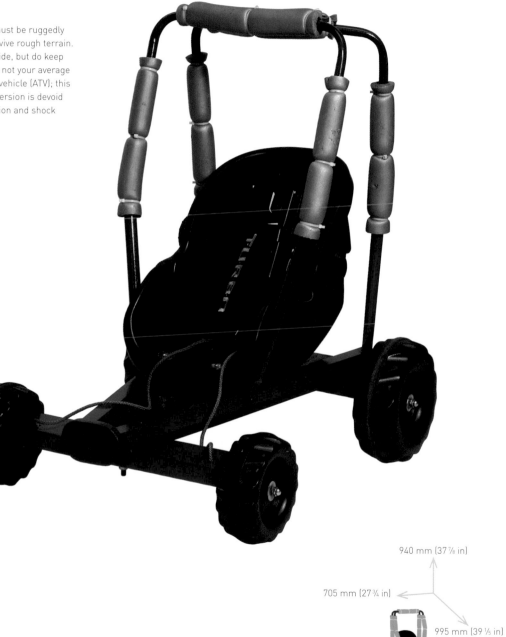

940 mm (37⅞ in)

705 mm (27¾ in)

995 mm (39⅛ in)

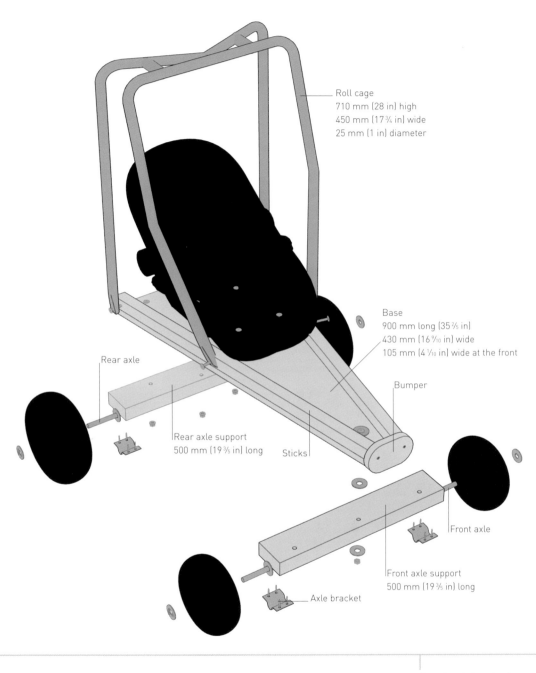

Roll cage
710 mm (28 in) high
450 mm (17¾ in) wide
25 mm (1 in) diameter

Base
900 mm long (35⅖ in)
430 mm (16⁹⁄₁₀ in) wide
105 mm (4¹⁄₁₀ in) wide at the front

Rear axle

Bumper

Rear axle support
500 mm (19⅗ in) long

Sticks

Front axle

Front axle support
500 mm (19⅗ in) long

Axle bracket

The chassis is a simple triangular shape, but the size and position of the roll cage is dependent on the design of the baby seat.

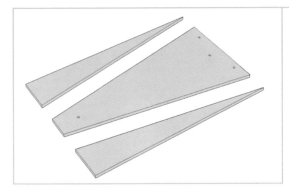

01 Use the tape measure, pencil, and a straight edge to mark out the almost triangular shape and cut that out with a jigsaw or handsaw. Keep the offcuts for something else. Drill a hole in the front for the front axle support pivot and three holes for bolts in the back for fixing the back axle support.

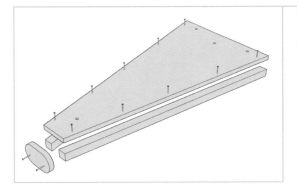

02 Turn the base over so you are working from the underside. Cut sticks with angled ends by copying the angle from the plywood, and fix these to the top side of the base with screws. You can use glue for extra strength. Cut and fix a rounded plywood bumper to the front.

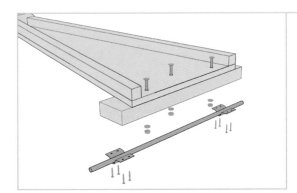

03 Bolt the back axle support to the base. Use washers underneath to spread the load. We have used metal brackets and screws to secure the axle to the support but you could instead use U bolts that wrap around the axle and bolt through the support. Don't fit wheels just yet, but you will need them now to work out how long your axles need to be. Allow enough length to go through the wheels, fit a washer each side of each wheel, and leave at least 10 mm (⅖ in) stub projecting out from the wheel to take the split pins. After cutting the axles to length, use a file to smooth the ends. The axle should be held firmly to the wood and not rotate.

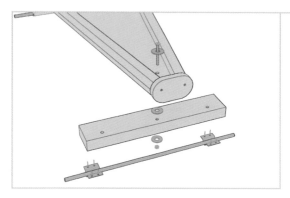

04 Prepare the front axle support with a hole for the pivot. This should be placed off-center to avoid the end of the bolt clashing with the centrally positioned axle. While you are at it, drill holes in the front axle support to take the steering/pulling rope. Bolt the base and axle support together using a large washer either side and in between to allow movement. Fix the front axle in the same way as the back and allow for sufficient length to go through each wheel.

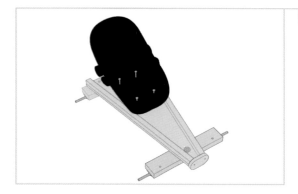

05 Fix the baby seat to the frame using four bolts, nuts, and washers. Before you fix on a position, try sitting in the seat and using the front axle support as a footrest. Move the seat backward or forward to find the ideal position, with knees slightly bent. Drill one hole through the seat and base at the same time and fix the first bolt. Check the seat position, drill the remaining holes, and fit the remaining screws.

06 The roll cage is made from a salvaged tubular steel chair frame plus extra lengths of tube bolted to it. You can also make it using new tube bent and welded to a similar shape. The precise shape will depend on your seat shell and the height of the person the cart is being built for. The cage should be a good 150 mm (6 in) higher than head height. We suggest trying the seat frame for size and possibly bending the legs a little by hand to meet your requirements. Hammer the ends of the tube flat, drill holes in the ends for bolts, file off sharp edges, and fix to the sides of the cart.

ROLL BARS

If you decide to design and build the roll bars yourself, you might consider including some side and front corner bars. Look at some professionally built ATVs for inspiration. Tube bending is good fun, but the kit is expensive and it's difficult to get the bends right first time. If you prefer, you can avoid welding the frame by using bolts to join the pieces together. (See the joins in the Wind-Powered Cart on page 136.)

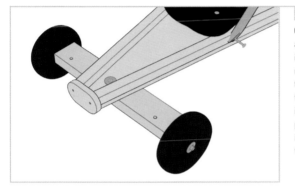

07 It is now a simple job to attach the wheels; drill holes in the ends of the axles to receive split pins, slide on the washers and wheels, and fit the split pins. Check all is working as expected and prepare to paint your cart. It is probably easier to remove the seat and wheels so you can sand and paint without damaging them. Attach a steering/pulling rope and pad the roll cage. For this we have used foam pipe insulation fixed with cable ties. After pulling up the cable ties, snip off the excess and file the ends smooth.

OFF-ROAD WHEELS

You need wheels with deep tread for this cart. This type of wheel can be difficult to find; try using those from a toddler's old mountain bike, or wheels from an old toy or discarded go-cart. You can buy wheels specially for off-road carts, but they are too expensive and quite frankly over-specified for this project. Our wheels do not have bearings, by the way—just holes in the middle.

The Three-Wheeled Cart

THREE-WHEELED CARTS HAVE A TENDENCY TO BE UNSTABLE, BUT THIS DESIGN ALLOWS THE DRIVER OPTIMUM CONTROL. The great advantage of three wheels is maneuverability; it's very easy to steer and you have a small turning circle. It's ideal for small yards and gardens. For this cart you really need the front part of an old children's bike.

YOU WILL NEED

Some basic tools:
- Tape measure
- Pencil
- Saw
- Drill/driver with bits
- Hacksaw
- File
- Pliers
- Coarse sandpaper
- A bench with a vise is useful, as is a metalwork vise

Some wood:
- You need pieces of strong plywood for the structure coming off the bike frame and the seat assembly

- The plywood could be salvaged, but as they are only small pieces why not splurge on new plywood for this project?
- If this is going to be a presentable gift you could use high-quality birch plywood, as that gives a smooth finish

Some metal:
- A 12 mm (½ in) diameter threaded rod, which you can buy from a DIY store, is ideal for the back axle and the front peg
- You will also need tubular steel that fits over that. It will act as "spacers" between the plywood shapes, and as sleeves for the foot pegs

You also need:
- The front part of a toddler's old broken bike—the smaller the better. Do make sure that the bike is definitely finished with and beyond repair—we got ours from a flea market
- Look out for two big bouncy wheels for the back

- Bearings are a bonus; we have used wheelbarrow wheels with no bearings
- You'll need to find a small bike wheel for the front. Use the one that came with the old bike if it's still okay. Our bike was too damaged, so we used a wheel from a good-quality but broken stroller

This cart is all about melding the front part of a bike with a plywood cart body and then bolting on big, funky wheels. You also need pegs at the front for your feet to rest on.

600 mm (23 ½ in)

570 mm (22 ⅖ in)　　　　1025 mm (40 ⅓ in)

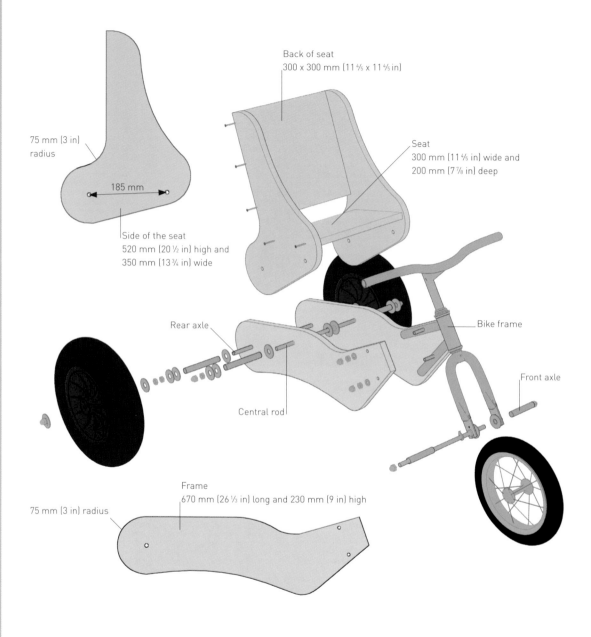

75 mm (3 in)
radius

185 mm

Side of the seat
520 mm (20 ½ in) high and
350 mm (13 ¾ in) wide

Back of seat
300 x 300 mm (11 ⅘ x 11 ⅘ in)

Seat
300 mm (11 ⅘ in) wide and
200 mm (7 ⅞ in) deep

Rear axle

Bike frame

Central rod

Front axle

75 mm (3 in) radius

Frame
670 mm (26 ⅓ in) long and 230 mm (9 in) high

The portion of bike is fixed
between layers of plywood.
The plywood shapes are
shown as templates; the
shapes are not critical, but
try to get smooth curves.

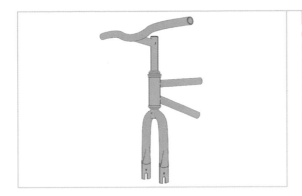

01 Use a hacksaw to cut through the bike frame in the region shown. The idea is to leave sufficient "stubs" for bolting in between the two layers of plywood. As soon as you have cut through the tube, file the ends smooth and keep the discarded part for cart spares. We have removed extraneous parts, but you could leave features like brakes, bells, and reflectors if they are any good.

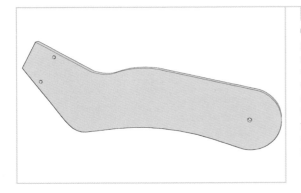

02 Plot the shape of the plywood frame onto the plywood using a tape measure, pencil, and compasses. Alternatively, draw round paint cans or a trashcan lid to get the curves you want. Cut out one with a jigsaw and sand the edges smooth. If the edges are a bit wobbly, try planing or filing them smooth. Reproduce the shape by drawing around it and cutting out again. Drill holes in the front for fixing to the bike frame and a hole in the back for the back axle. It is better to leave the other hole —for linking the front of the seat—until later, when you can mark it accurately.

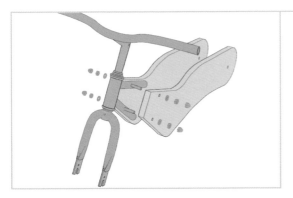

03 If you have a G-clamp, use it to hold one side of the plywood frame in position on the bike frame and drill through the holes in the plywood and through the bike frame. Use bolts, nuts, and washers to fix the plywood to the bike frame.

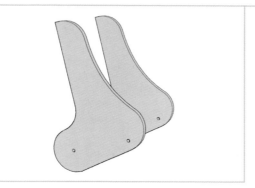

04 Mark out the shape of the sides of the seat onto plywood. Again, these are not critical and in fact you may want to adjust these for a smaller child or a more laid-back angle. When you have cut one out, use it as a template for producing the second.

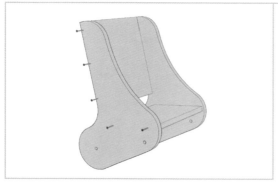

05 Cut the rectangular seat and back pieces and use screws and glue to join the seat shell parts together. Allow the glue to dry and sand off any sharp or rough edges.

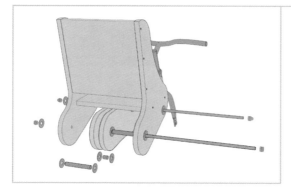

06 Place the seat shell over the plywood frame and insert a rod through the back axle holes to fix the position of the seat. This is a good time to work out the finished lengths of the axle and central rod; cut them to length and file the ends smooth. Mark the location of the remaining hole in the plywood frame for the central rod. Remove the seat from the frame and drill the last holes. Now you can thread the axle and central rod through the holes in the plywood frame. As you do, include the washers and tube spacers. Finish with nuts either side of the seat. Check that equal lengths of rod project either side and tighten.

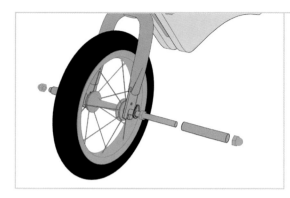

07 The front foot pegs are made from a single length of rod, about 300 mm (1 ft) long. The rod needs to fit through the wheel. If you are using a bike wheel, undo the nuts either side of the wheel and remove the bearings and bolt. If the rod is a loose fit in the wheel you can make a tube sleeve to improve the fit, but the wheel does need to move freely. Follow the diagram when fittting the rod. You need location washers—these are washers that come with the bike. A tab on the washer locates in a hole in the fork and prevents the wheel from slipping out. Check the rod is central and make tube sleeves to fit over the rod on both sides. Tighten the nuts at the ends and both sides of the forks.

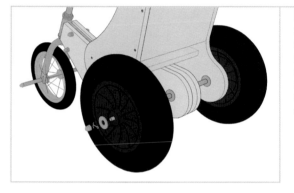

08 Drill holes for split pins in the ends of the back axle and fit the wheels. Bend over the ends of the pin. For a better finish, add a dome nut to the end of the rod. Test the cart. If it all works, prepare for painting. We have used fluorescent colors, and for this you need to start with a white base coat. For best results, take the cart apart and paint the pieces individually.

PEDAL OPTION

With a little extra work this can be a pedal go-cart. Instead of a straight rod for the foot pegs, make a bent (cranked) rod with pedals on. You would need to work out a way of fixing the wheel to the crank. This could be washer- or plate-welded to the crank and then fixed to the wheel hub with bolts, or you could tack-weld the hub to the crank on both sides. An alternative that may be easier is to find a broken toy with a wheel, crank, and pedals and see if that will fit into your forks.

The Dragster

DRAGSTERS ARE PROBABLY THE FASTEST-
ACCELERATING VEHICLES ON EARTH; QUICKER
EVEN THAN THE SPACE SHUTTLE LAUNCHER
OR JET FIGHTER. Well, this isn't that fast, but it
does have some of that dragster styling: long, thin,
streamlined body, big slicks on the back, plenty of
chrome, and flames licking up the sides.

YOU WILL NEED

Some basic tools:
- A tape measure
- Pencil
- Jigsaw
- Drill/driver with bits
- Hacksaw
- File
- Pliers
- Coarse sandpaper.
- A bench with a vise
  will make things a lot
  easier

Some wood:
- You need long pieces
  of strong plywood for
  the boxlike structure.

These could be
salvaged plywood, but
make sure you have
the good face outward,
otherwise you could
be faced with a lot of
sanding and filling
- For the curved top/
  front of the car you
  need 4–6 mm (¼ in)
  thin, flexible plywood

Some metal:
- 12 mm (½ in) diameter
  axles are okay—buy
  them from a DIY store
- Nuts

- Bolts
- Washers

You also need:
- We have used smooth
  wheelbarrow wheels
  for the back and
  thinner bike wheels
  of a similar diameter
  for the front, none of
  which use bearings
- If you are going to
  race, then find wheels
  with roller bearing
  or bearings and stub
  axles that you can use
  instead
- Bike wheels can

be used with their
bearings if you can
weld stubs to the end
or, even better, an axle
linking the wheels
- The eye bolt, racing
  mesh (metal on the
  sloping surface), and
  aluminum trim are
  expensive options.
  You could instead do a
  brilliant paint job with
  go-faster stripes

This is a great cart shape for racing straight courses, but it is no good for tight turns. It is easily big enough for three or four kids; one in the seat, one on the top bit and one or two in front.

680 mm (26 ¾ in)

590 mm (23 ⅛ in)

1920 mm (75 ⅗ in)

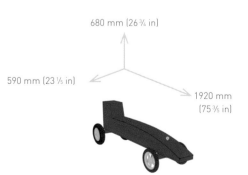

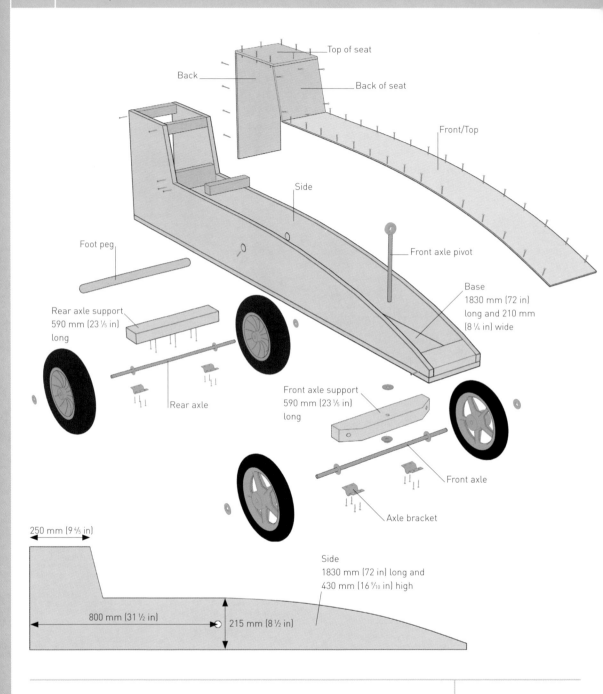

Top of seat

Back

Back of seat

Front/Top

Side

Front axle pivot

Foot peg

Base
1830 mm (72 in)
long and 210 mm
(8 ¼ in) wide

Rear axle support
590 mm (23 ⅕ in)
long

Front axle support
590 mm (23 ⅕ in)
long

Rear axle

Front axle

Axle bracket

250 mm (9 ⅘ in)

Side
1830 mm (72 in) long and
430 mm (16 ⁹⁄₁₀ in) high

800 mm (31 ½ in)

215 mm (8 ½ in)

The boxlike structure is
incredibly strong. It is achieved
using thick plywood for the
base and sides "skinned" with
thin plywood.

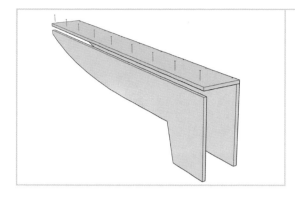

01 Mark out the shape of a side onto thick plywood using a tape measure, pencil, and straight edge. We marked out a smooth curve using the sheet of thin bendy plywood as a template. This is easier if you can get someone to bend the ply to a suitable curve. Cut out and smooth the edges with a plane and use the finished shape as a template for the other side. Cut out the rectangular base and use glue and screws to fix it to the sides.

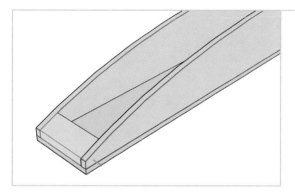

02 Cut a piece of pine to fit between the sides at the front of the cart and mark the shape of the sides onto the ends so you know what needs cutting away. Fix this with glue and screws. When the glue is dry, check the block finishes flush with the sides and make any adjustments using a plane.

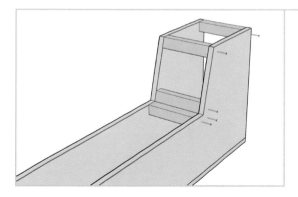

03 Link the sides at the corners as shown using lengths of batten, glue, and screws. Check they are positioned accurately (angled and aligned with the plywood). These sticks form the corners and support the thinner plywood "skin."

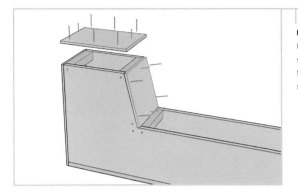

04 Use glue and nails to fix the end, top, and back-of-seat areas of thin plywood to the crosspieces and plywood sides.

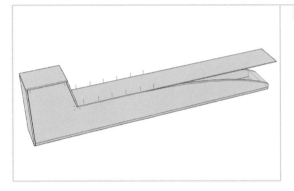

05 For the curved front/top of the cart, cut a piece of thin plywood larger than required; about 4 mm (¼ in) larger all around. Starting at the top, glue and nail it to the wood crosspieces and plywood sides. When the glue has dried, trim off the excess flush with the sides using a plane.

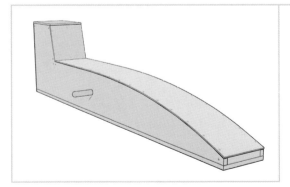

06 Fit the foot pegs to the cart. This is a single piece of thick dowel—a piece of broom stick is about right—located in holes and fixed with glue and nails driven at a suitable angle. Round over the ends of the dowel.

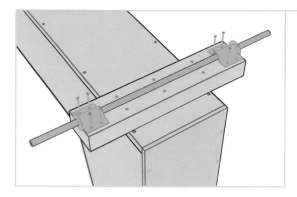

07 Turn the cart over and glue and screw the back axle support somewhere near to the back of the cart. Work out the length of axle required by loading on the washers and wheels and allowing 10 mm (⅖ in)-long stubs sticking out for the split pins to go through. Cut the axle to length and file the ends smooth. At this stage you can also drill holes for the split pins. Fix the axle using brackets at either end of the axle support.

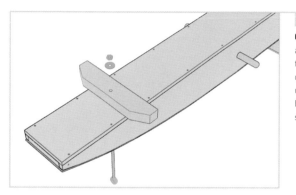

08 Drill a hole for the front axle pivot right through the cart—you may have to drill from both sides; mark up accurately so the holes line up. Make the front axle support; this is the same as the back one but with shaped ends. Drill a pivot hole in the support making it slightly off-center so that the bolt does not clash with the axle. Bolt on the front axle support and make sure it pivots freely.

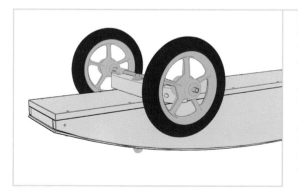

09 As you did for the back of the cart, work out the length of the front axle, cut and drill holes for the split pins, and attach it to the support. Fit the wheels and test the cart. Remove the wheels and sand smooth, making sure you round over corners and edges. Paint black and then add red and yellow flames using spray paint and a flame-shaped stencil cut from thin card, and allowing the paint to dry before reusing the stencil. You could also paint on flames by hand. Add the optional trim; the racing mesh is from a car spares store and the aluminum section is from a DIY store. Fix both with screws set in screw cups.

The Two-Man Cart

THAT'S RIGHT, NOW YOU DON'T HAVE TO GO IT
ALONE! Make this cart with your friend and go racing
together. The driver in front has the steering and
the one in the back has the brakes. This is an ideal
racer for your local derby, but, as with all designs,
you need to check on the race rules before starting to
build.

YOU WILL NEED

Some basic tools:
- Tape measure
- Pencil
- Jigsaw
- Drill/driver with bits
- Hacksaw
- File
- Pliers
- Coarse sandpaper
- A workbench of some description is needed

Some wood:
- This monocoque (single shell) design starts with a thick, sturdy plywood base and back
- Battens are added around the edges and the cart is "skinned" with thin, bendy plywood
- This ply and the other solid wood pieces are available from DIY stores

Some metal:
- 12 mm (½ in) diameter axles from a DIY store or metal supplier
- Nuts
- Bolts
- Washers
- Brackets
- We have finished the exposed plywood edges with U-section aluminum trim glued with epoxy resin, but this is an optional extra

You also need:
- A set of good wheels. We found these solid rubber wheels in a DIY store; they are the type often used on hand carts. These are great race wheels because they come complete with roller bearings and won't let you down

This cart has two comfortable seats, rope steering coming through the dashboard, and brakes. All of this, complete with a stylish streamlined body shell. Finish off with a silver front, mirrors, and metal edge trim.

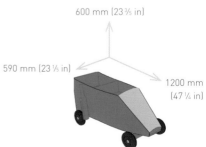

600 mm (23 ⅜ in)

590 mm (23 ⅕ in)

1200 mm (47 ¼ in)

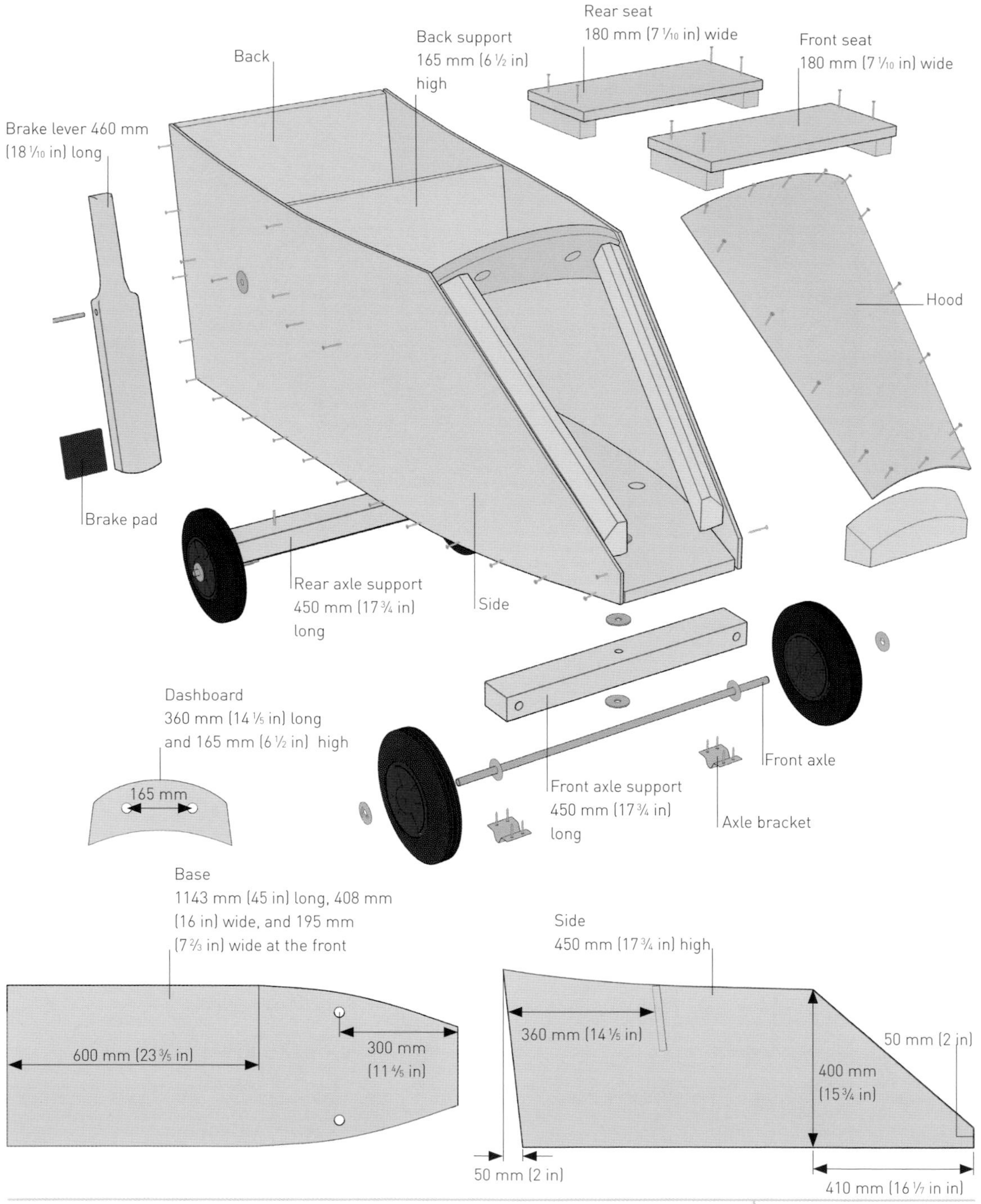
Back
Back support
165 mm (6 1/2 in)
high
Rear seat
180 mm (7 1/10 in) wide
Front seat
180 mm (7 1/10 in) wide
Brake lever 460 mm
(18 1/10 in) long
Hood
Brake pad
Rear axle support
450 mm (17 3/4 in)
long
Side
Dashboard
360 mm (14 1/5 in) long
and 165 mm (6 1/2 in) high
165 mm
Front axle
Front axle support
450 mm (17 3/4 in)
long
Axle bracket
Base
1143 mm (45 in) long, 408 mm
(16 in) wide, and 195 mm
(7 2/3 in) wide at the front
600 mm (23 3/5 in)
300 mm
(11 4/5 in)
Side
450 mm (17 3/4 in) high
360 mm (14 1/5 in)
50 mm (2 in)
400 mm
(15 3/4 in)
50 mm (2 in)
410 mm (16 1/7 in in)

Here you can see how both the sides and the hood follow smooth curves.

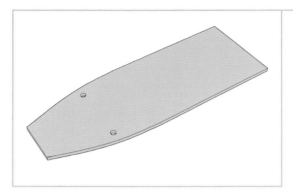

01 Mark out the shape of the base on to thick plywood using a tape measure, pencil, and straight edge. Mark the curve using a piece of bendy ply as a template. Ask someone to bend and hold the ply while you draw the curve. Mark one side only, cut off the excess with the jigsaw, and use the offcut—flipped over the other way—to mark a symmetrical curve on the other side. Finish cutting and smooth the edges if necessary with a plan. Drill the two holes for the rope steering in the base of the cart.

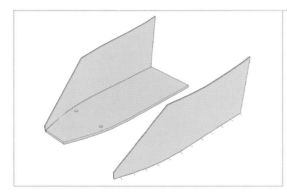

02 Cut out the two side panels from thin, bendy plywood. Use the template opposite as a guide to the shape required, but it is best to make the shape over length—measure around the curve on your base; about 25 mm (1 in) longer is about right. Glue and pin the sides to the base, starting at the back, with the corners perfectly aligned, and finishing at the front. Trim off the excess plywoood that extends at the front using a saw and plane.

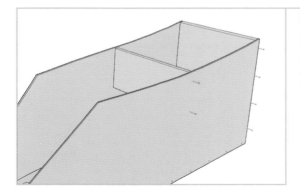

03 Now cut a thick plywood back to fit in the space between the sides, and a smaller piece of thick ply for the driver's back support. Fix these with glue and screws.

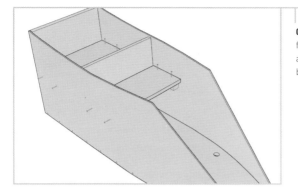

04 Cut more pieces of thick ply for the front and back seats and fix them to the sides using battens, glue, and screws.

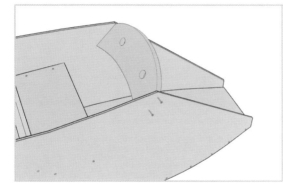

05 Follow the template on page 66 for producing the dashboard. You will need to plane off some material from either end to match the angles of the sides. This is best done gradually; keep checking the fit as you go. Drill two holes in the dashboard for the steering rope. Fix using glue and screws at approximately 45°, although this angle is just a guide—it is not critical.

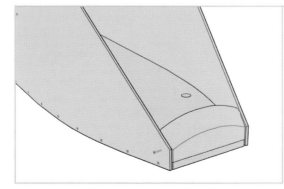

06 Now you need to fill in the nose of the cart with a shaped block of wood. This shape not only reinforces the front of the cart, it also sets the shape of the curved hood and gives you something to fix the hood to. Cut a generous block of wood that fits between the sides, mark the angle of the side onto the end of the block, and copy the curve from the dashboard onto the front of the block. Use these marks as a guide when you remove the excess material. Set the jigsaw to a corresponding angle. Fix the block with glue and screws.

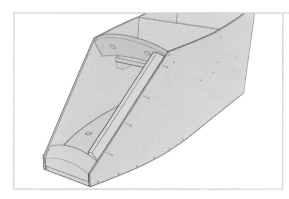

07 Battens are needed to support the sides of the hood; these need to be planed to an angled shape that corresponds roughly to the curve of the dashboard. Fix these with more glue and screws.

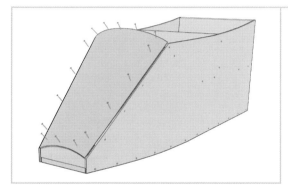

08 Now the fun bit: bending and fixing the hood. We suggest you use good-quality plywood with the grain running lengthways (see below). Cut the plywood about 6 mm (¼ in) larger than you need. Place the plywood over the cart, ask someone to bend it to shape, and mark around it with a pencil. Apply glue to the edges to be joined, ask for help again bending the wood, and fix with screws. We drilled countersunk holes to give a better finish. After the glue has dried, plane off the overhanging plywood so it finishes flush.

BENDING PLYWOOD

This is nothing to be feared, but it works best if you use good-quality plywood as it is more flexible. The best plywood for this job is birch plywood, but other kinds are okay. You can only bend plywood one way—a bit like a piece of card; you can have several curves in one piece but you can't make a dome shape (compound curve), for example—so you need to check your curves are achievable. For very tight curves, you can build up (laminate) several layers of very thin ply (aero ply), or perhaps sheet metal.

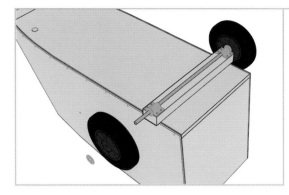

09 Screw and glue the back axle support to the underside of the cart and prepare to fit the back axle. Measure how long your axle needs to be (the front axle will be the same); thread on the wheels and washers, and allow for a 10 mm (⅖ in) stub sticking out from the wheels to drill and insert a split pin. Cut the axle to length, round over the ends with a file, and drill the holes for the split pins. Fit to the cart using brackets and screws. Attach the wheels.

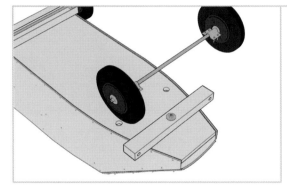

10 Pivot the front axle support to the cart using a bolt, washers, and a nut. The pivot hole in the support should be either off-center or recessed to avoid clashing with the axle that runs through the center. Prepare and fix the axle in the same way as for the back and attach the wheels. Drill holes through the ends of the axle support to take the steering rope.

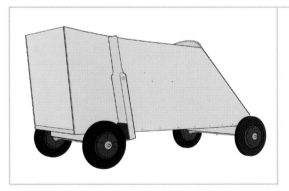

11 Make a brake lever and fix it to the side. The brake pad can be a chunk of rubber, if you can find one, or else use a folded pad of old bike tire. Thread the steering rope through the axle support, up through the base and dashboard, and back down the other side, and put a knot in the ends to stop it pulling out. Test your cart. When you are happy, prepare to paint it. Sand off all the sharp edges and bring it to a good finish. Remove the rope and wheels before you paint.

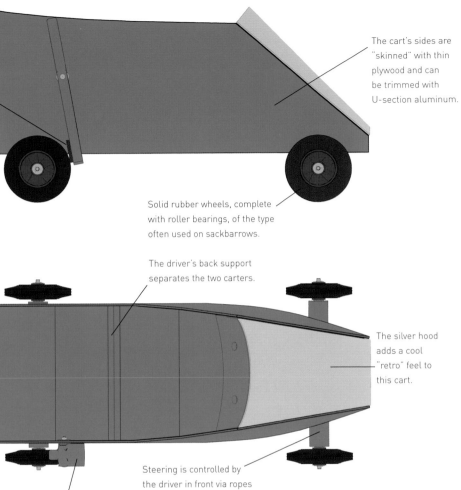

A brake pad made from a chunk of rubber; perhaps a few thicknesses of an old bike tire glued together

The cart's sides are "skinned" with thin plywood and can be trimmed with U-section aluminum.

Solid rubber wheels, complete with roller bearings, of the type often used on sackbarrows.

The driver's back support separates the two carters.

The silver hood adds a cool "retro" feel to this cart.

The person at the back controls the braking via a single lever.

Steering is controlled by the driver in front via ropes attached to the front axle.

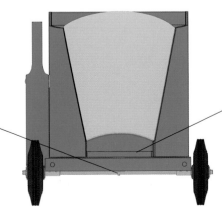

The pivot hole for the front axle is either set off-center or recessed to avoid clashing with the axle.

A specially shaped wooden block serves to reinforce the front of the cart and also sets the curve of the hood.

The Racing Cart

AWE SPECTATORS WITH THIS FORMULA 1-STYLE DREAM MACHINE. This is another derby race cart that is not just about speed; appearance is paramount. Spoilers (wings) and big wheels are the main features of the highest class of racing autos, so we have included those here, plus a fancy air intake and some metallic pipes.

YOU WILL NEED

Some basic tools:
- A workbench and vise will prove indispensable
- A sturdy surface to work on and some clamps to hold the work down
- Tape measure
- Compass
- Pencil
- Jigsaw
- Drill/driver with drill and screwdriver bits
- Hacksaw
- File
- Pliers

Some wood:
- The floor, sides, back end, spoilers, and steering mechanism underneath are made from strong plywood
- The floor and steering components are out of sight so can be rough plywood, but the rest is on display and should be good quality
- If you are going to enter it in a race, build quality is important, so get the best materials
- The front axle support is made of pine, as are the various sections used in the construction (see the exploded diagram on page 74)
- The hood is made from flexible plywood. Quality varies, but we suggest using birch plywood as it is smooth and flexible

Some metal:
- The axles are dependent on your wheels, but if you have a choice, go for 13 mm (½ in) diameter solid steel axles
- For the steering column you can use a thinner diameter

You also need:
- Wheels with pneumatic tires, and preferably bearings— roller bearings or those with axle stubs or stubs welded on—are needed, plus a plastic seat, steering wheel, and some plastic plumbing pipes or other suitable accessories
- Brakes are necessary; they can be calipers or plunger type

This monocoque design features a strong plywood floor panel, profiled sides, and is "skinned" with a flexible plywood hood. This is a heavy beast and could easily hold two kids if the seat were turned into a bench. You need four bike wheels, with slightly larger ones for the back.

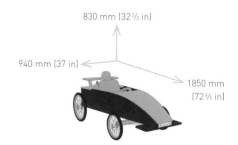

830 mm (32⅔ in)

940 mm (37 in)

1850 mm (72⅘ in)

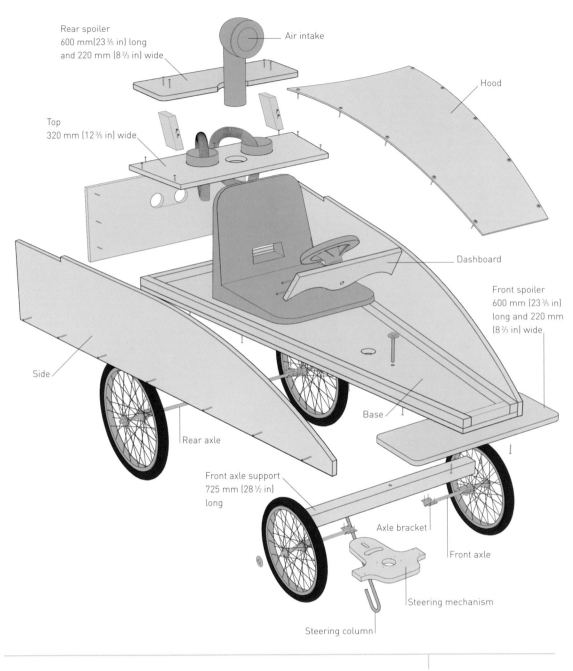

Rear spoiler
600 mm (23 ⅗ in) long
and 220 mm (8 ⅔ in) wide

Air intake

Hood

Top
320 mm (12 ⅗ in) wide

Dashboard

Front spoiler
600 mm (23 ⅗ in)
long and 220 mm
(8 ⅔ in) wide

Side

Rear axle

Base

Front axle support
725 mm (28 ½ in)
long

Axle bracket

Front axle

Steering mechanism

Steering column

This exploded view clearly
shows the shell construction
and steering mechanism. The
pipes at the back are optional.

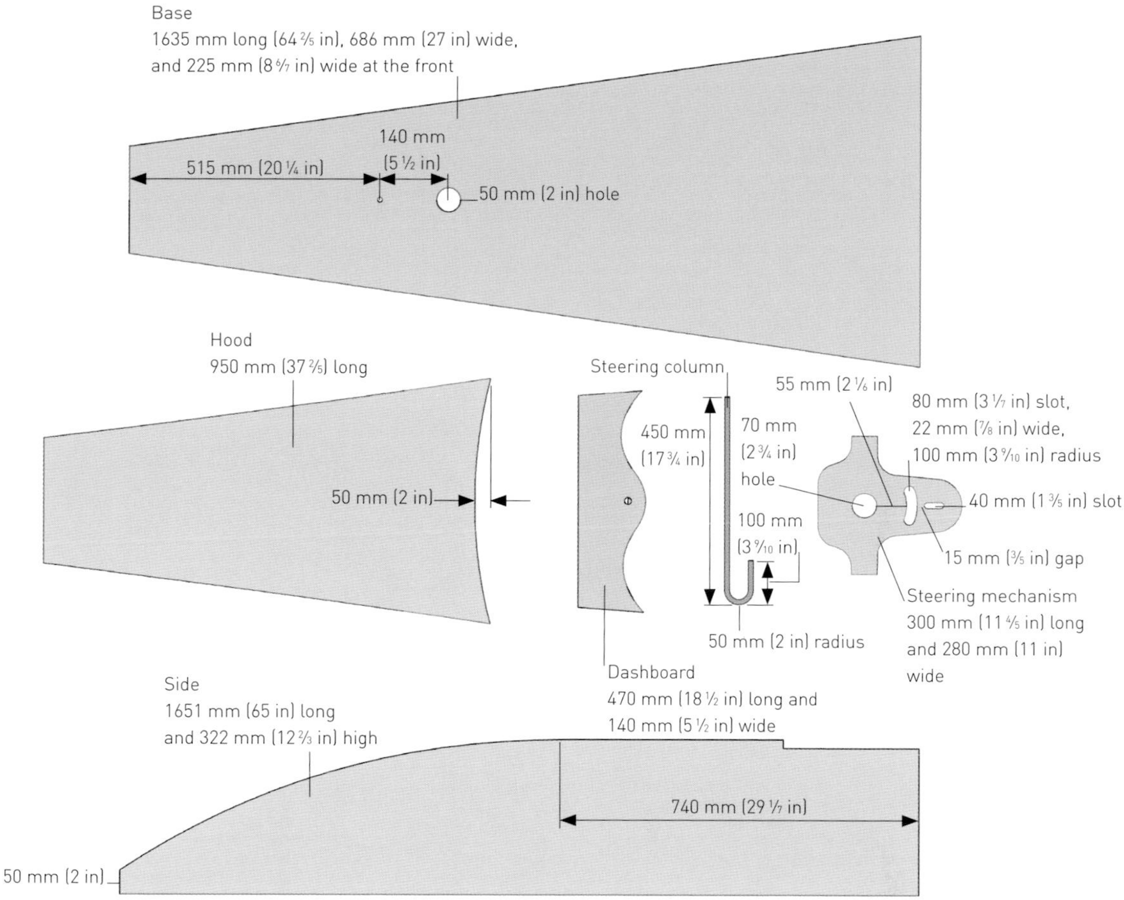
Base
1635 mm long (64 2/5 in), 686 mm (27 in) wide, and 225 mm (8 6/7 in) wide at the front
140 mm (5 1/2 in)
515 mm (20 1/4 in)
50 mm (2 in) hole
Hood
950 mm (37 2/5) long
50 mm (2 in)
Steering column
450 mm (17 3/4 in)
70 mm (2 3/4 in) hole
100 mm (3 9/10 in)
50 mm (2 in) radius
55 mm (2 1/6 in)
80 mm (3 1/7 in) slot, 22 mm (7/8 in) wide, 100 mm (3 9/10 in) radius
40 mm (1 3/5 in) slot
15 mm (3/5 in) gap
Steering mechanism
300 mm (11 4/5 in) long and 280 mm (11 in) wide
Dashboard
470 mm (18 1/2 in) long and 140 mm (5 1/2 in) wide
Side
1651 mm (65 in) long and 322 mm (12 2/3 in) high
740 mm (29 1/7 in)
50 mm (2 in)

Templates for the cart. The hood should be treated as a guide only. Cut oversize and trim to fit.

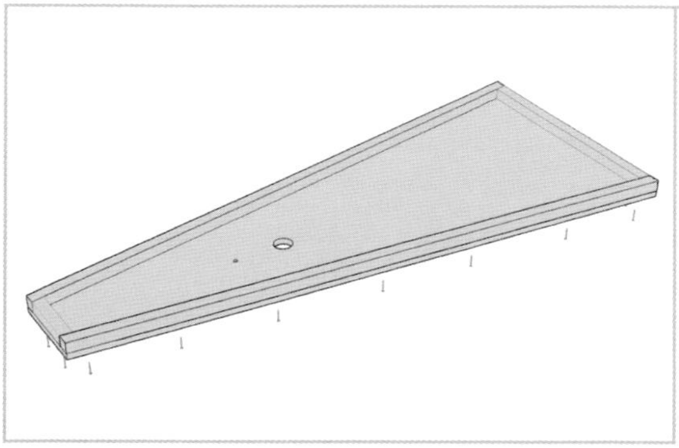

01 Cut out the floor panel. This is a simple almost-triangular shape (see the template above). Drill the large steering-column hole with a holesaw and cut a smaller hole for the front axle pivot. Screw and glue sticks all around as shown.

02 Follow the template on page 75 when marking out the shape of the sides. The step at the back is for a plywood "lid," so make it match the thickness of your plywood. Ask a friend to flex a length of thin plywood to create a smooth curve to draw around. The curve is not critical, but the point at which the curve begins is important to note. After cutting one side, use it as a template for producing the other side. Sand smooth and fix to the floor panel with glue and screws, making sure that the screws go into the sticks rather than the thickness of the plywood.

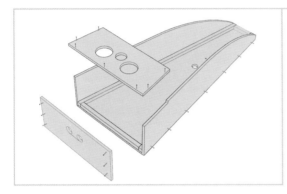

03 Cut out the boards for the back end of the cart. The holes are for the optional pipes. If you are going to include those, first make a trip to a DIY store or plumber's supplier and choose some funky pipes. Drill or cut suitably sized holes so that the pipes are a wedge-tight fit. A holesaw will make the smaller holes nicely; for the larger holes, draw around the pipes and cut out the waste with a jigsaw. Sand smooth before screwing and gluing.

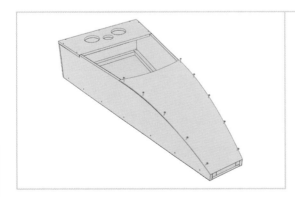

04 The hood should be cut from thin plywood slightly oversize 5 mm (¼ in) all around, except on the curved side facing the driver. Ask a friend to bend the sheet over the curve and hold it still while you mark around the front of the shape with a pencil. Cut out and, again with help, apply glue and bend it to fit. Fix with countersunk screws set in screw cups for a good finish. When dry, plane off the excess overhanging wood until it is flush with the sides of the cart. Add some aluminum U-shaped trim to the side facing the driver if you wish.

05 Work out the length of axle required at the back. Mount the wheels including washers and leave a stub of 10 mm (⅜ in) projecting either end for the split pins. Cut the axle to length and file the ends smooth. Fix the back axle somewhere near to the back of the cart. Use three strong brackets and screw them down tightly to prevent the axle from turning.

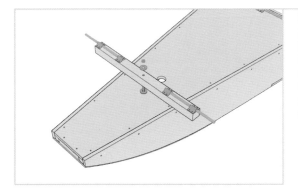

06 Work out the length of the front axle stubs at the front. The gap in between is to allow for the steering mechanism. Again, position wheels and washers and allow for extra at the ends. Make a front axle support and drill a center hole. Attach this to the predrilled hole in the cart floor with a bolt and washers. Fix the axles with brackets and screws.

AXLE FIXINGS

Here you have a number of choices. First, an even stronger alternative to brackets are U bolts, but these are less easy to obtain and not so easy to fit. Alternatively, you can stay with the brackets but fix them with nuts and bolts instead of screws. If you are a bit crafty, you can use square-section metal with lathe-turned ends that fit the bearings in your wheels, and bolt those securely to the floor panel. If your wheels have stub axles, the U bolts are probably the best choice, or else weld long stubs to wheel spindles or an axle in between.

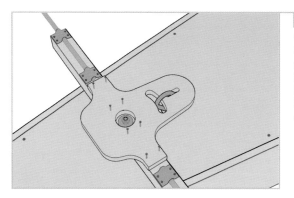

07 Cut out the steering mechanism as accurately as you can. The outline is not important, but the shapes of the slots and the distances between the slots and pivot are critical. Screw it into position on the axle support, making sure that the hole fits around the bolt, washer, and nut. Make a steering rod with a crook end and insert that up through the cart.

STEERING OPTIONS

You could opt for cable steering in this cart instead of the mechanism shown (see the Soapbox Racer on page 82). You may need to do that if race rules dictate "non-mechanical steering," even though that definition is obviously unclear. Check this out with the race organizers. You need a much thicker steering column for cable steering; a cart of this weight needs thick cable and tension devices, as discussed in the Soapbox Racer project.

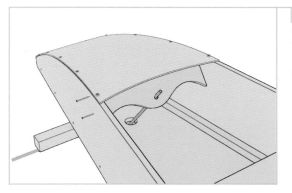

08 Make a dashboard (see the template on page 75) to fit in between the sides. This has a dual purpose. The steering rod is supported by it and it fits up to and reinforces the hood area near the driver. The wavy shape makes room for the driver's legs.

BRAKE OPTIONS

We chose to mount linear-pull caliper bike brakes on both front wheels, mainly because they look cool and are very effective. These can be found on an old bike. They require additional strong metal brackets made to a suitable height and mounted on top of the axle support. Run the cables through the side of the cart into the cabin and into a single brake lever. Spend time adjusting the brakes so they pull evenly on both sides. This is difficult but necessary; otherwise, the steering will be affected when braking.

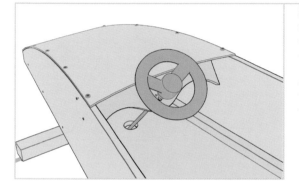

09 Attach a ready-made steering wheel to the top of the rod using a washer between it and the dashboard and a retaining screw passing through the steering wheel and into the rod.

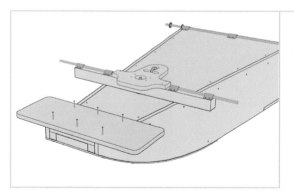

10 Cut a front spoiler from strong plywood (kids might step on this, so thin ply is no good), give it rounded corners, and sand smooth. Fit to the underside of the cart using six screws, four of which can run into the solid wood sticks running down the side of the cart.

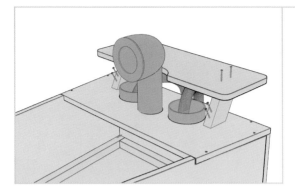

11 The rear spoiler is identical in shape and is mounted on angled blocks to give it a more streamlined effect and make room for the "air intake." Fix the angled blocks as shown or from underneath if you don't mind fiddling around in the cramped space. Use four long screws to fit the spoiler to the blocks. Glue is of little advantage here, as the end grain does not stick well—just make sure the screws are adequate.

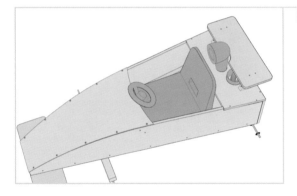

12 Fit a plastic chair seat in the cockpit. Bolt this to the floor using four bolts or, as shown here, screw from underneath into the ready-made lugs in the seat.

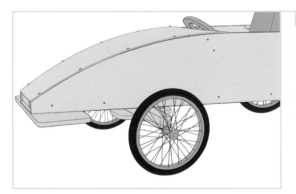

13 Fit the wheels with washers either side and a split pin to hold them on. Test drive. If all is working correctly, you can prepare to paint. Remove the wheels and other parts that you want to paint separately. Sand the surfaces smooth and apply a coat of paint. Allow to dry, lightly sand to remove any lumps and bumps, and recoat. Reassemble when you are sure all the paintwork is dry.

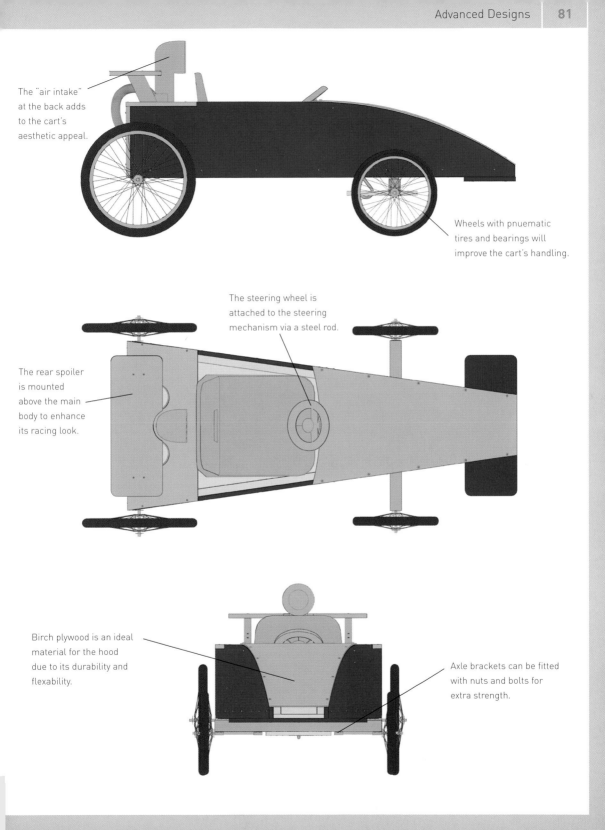

The "air intake" at the back adds to the cart's aesthetic appeal.

Wheels with pnuematic tires and bearings will improve the cart's handling.

The steering wheel is attached to the steering mechanism via a steel rod.

The rear spoiler is mounted above the main body to enhance its racing look.

Birch plywood is an ideal material for the hood due to its durability and flexability.

Axle brackets can be fitted with nuts and bolts for extra strength.

The Soapbox Racer

THIS STYLE OF CART HAS EVOLVED OVER MANY DECADES AND IS TYPICALLY USED IN SOAP BOX DERBY RACES. Its simple streamlined shape harks back to 1950s racing cars; if you can find some 1950s stroller wheels to go with it, then you are well away. If you are going to build this cart for racing in a local derby, check out their rules before you start.

YOU WILL NEED

Some basic tools:
- Jigsaw
- Drill/driver with drill and screwdriver bits
- A hacksaw
- File
- Pliers
- A workbench and vise will make your work more enjoyable

Some wood:
- The floor and top are two identical shapes of thick, strong plywood
- The floor is not seen, so can be rough

plywood, but the top is on display and should be good quality. If it's going to be varnished then you have even more reason to pick something decorative
- Races are judged on build quality as well as speed, so maybe you should splurge on this one. A covering of walnut veneer, for example, would look fabulous
- The axle supports are made of pine, but

for an even stronger, sleeker model try using a hardwood like ash or hickory
- The sides are made from flexible plywood. Again, quality varies, but we suggest using birch plywood, which is extremely smooth and flexible

Some metal:
- The axles are dependent on your wheels; if you have a choice, go for

13 mm (½ in) diameter solid stainless-steel axles. Making all your other fixings from stainless steel will prevent rust. Use only nylon-insert locking nuts.

You also need:
- Choose your wheels carefully. Our wheels are from an old stroller and work fine
- Race winners these days use top-quality bearings and pneumatic tires

This classic monocoque design is well balanced and easy to control. The cable steering is designed for derby racing, particularly for long downhill stretches. The brake is a lever in the floor that pushes a pad against the ground.

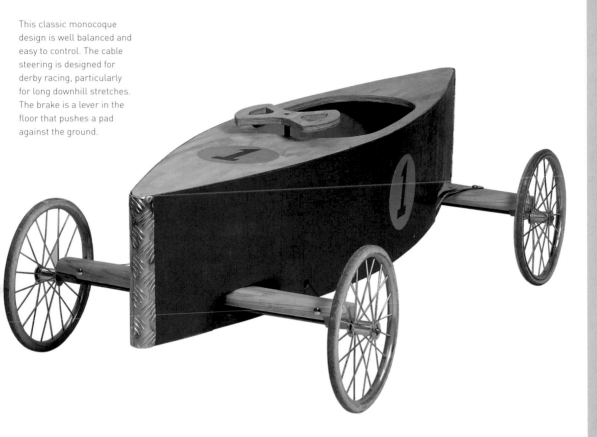

500 mm (19⅔ in)

800 mm (31½ in)

1565 mm (61⅗ in)

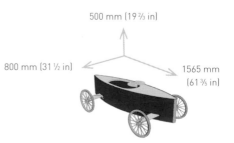

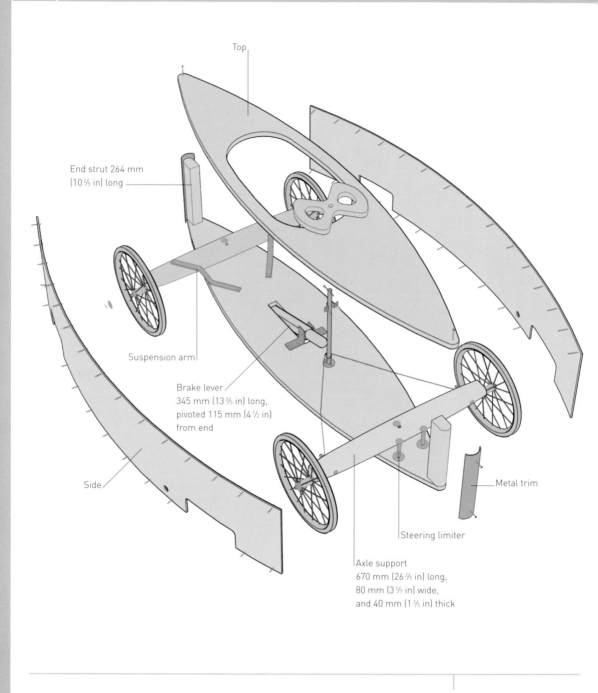

Top

End strut 264 mm
(10 2/5 in) long

Suspension arm

Brake lever
345 mm (13 3/5 in) long,
pivoted 115 mm (4 1/2 in)
from end

Side

Metal trim

Steering limiter

Axle support
670 mm (26 2/5 in) long,
80 mm (3 1/2 in) wide,
and 40 mm (1 3/5 in) thick

Here you can see all the
workings of the cart; the back
axle suspension, the brake,
and the cable steering and
steering limiters.

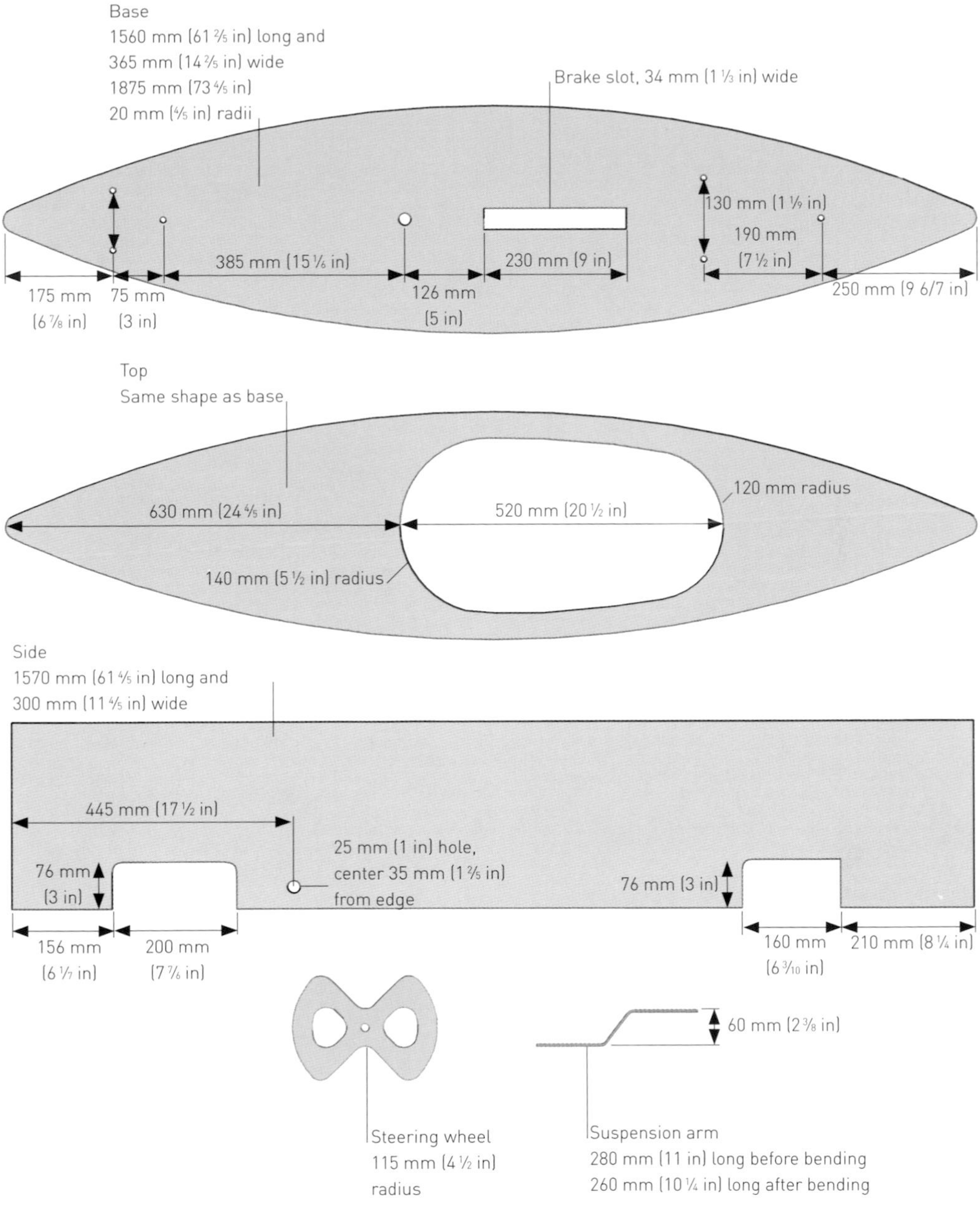
Base
1560 mm (61 2/5 in) long and
365 mm (14 2/5 in) wide
1875 mm (73 4/5 in)
20 mm (4/5 in) radii
Brake slot, 34 mm (1 1/3 in) wide
130 mm (1 1/9 in)
190 mm
(7 1/2 in)
385 mm (15 1/6 in)
230 mm (9 in)
175 mm
(6 7/8 in)
75 mm
(3 in)
126 mm
(5 in)
250 mm (9 6/7 in)
Top
Same shape as base
120 mm radius
630 mm (24 4/5 in)
520 mm (20 1/2 in)
140 mm (5 1/2 in) radius
Side
1570 mm (61 4/5 in) long and
300 mm (11 4/5 in) wide
445 mm (17 1/2 in)
25 mm (1 in) hole,
center 35 mm (1 2/5 in)
from edge
76 mm
(3 in)
76 mm (3 in)
156 mm
(6 1/7 in)
200 mm
(7 7/8 in)
160 mm
(6 3/10 in)
210 mm (8 1/4 in)
60 mm (2 3/8 in)
Steering wheel
115 mm (4 1/2 in)
radius
Suspension arm
280 mm (11 in) long before bending
260 mm (10 1/4 in) long after bending

Templates for the plywood components. The steering wheel can be substituted for a metal version. The suspension bar is shown in profile.

SHAPE, SIZE, AND WEIGHT

It is easy to modify the dimensions to suit your requirements. Race rules vary and you must comply with dimensions and weight. Normally the aim is to make the shell as small and streamlined as possible but to make it up to the maximum weight allowable. You can add weights to the floor, but why not use that weight for adding strength? Among other factors you should check are length, width, wheelbase, wheel diameter, ground clearance, braking method (brakes are always required), and steering method.

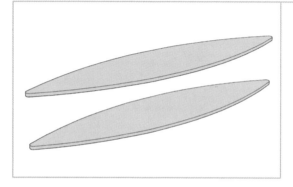

01 Mark out the shape of the floor panel—and the identical top panel—using the template on page 85, a tape measure, and pencil. The curve is not critical but does need to be symmetrical. We suggest asking a friend to help you by bending a piece of thin plywood to the required curve while you mark it. If you mark and cut just half of one side you can use the offcut as a template for marking out the rest of the shape. For a good finish, plane the edges to the smoothest curve possible.

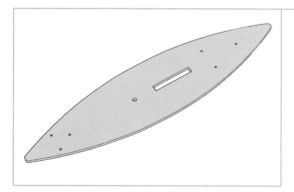

02 Now concentrate on the floor board. Again, follow the template on page 85, which shows you where to drill the holes in the front for the front axle pivot and steering limiter bolts, and the holes in the back for the back axle fixing point and suspension. The hole near the center is for the steering column. The slot is for the brake lever; make a big hole somewhere in the middle of the slot for entering the blade of the jigsaw. Sand the edges and surfaces to a smooth finish, but don't go too far.

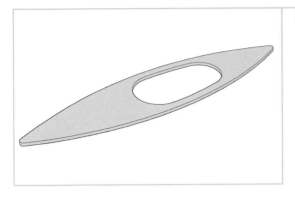

03 The hole for your body is marked out using a compass and tape measure. Follow the template on page 85. Basically, it is a big circle merged into a smaller circle, but the thin portions left and right are not straight lines linking the circles but run parallel with the sides. Use a small scrap of wood, the same width as the margin around the hole, and a pencil aligned with the end to scribe the shape. Sand the wood smooth.

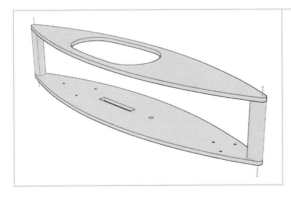

04 Find two chunks of wood that can be used for end struts. They need not be the highest quality as they will be covered up by the metal trim. You might want to miss out the trim and make them a decorative feature—if so, they need to be shaped and finished to a high standard. As it is, ours are covered, so mark out the shape using one of the boards as a rough template and plane them to meet the curve. Use glue and two countersunk screws at each end to fix the boards to the struts. For a better finish, you can recess the screw heads and plug the holes with wooden plugs to match the top surface.

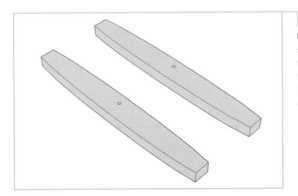

05 Produce two identical axle supports with holes near the centers for fixing to the floor board. Note that the holes should be positioned off-center to allow for the axle to pass centrally. Alternative options are to recess the axle in the support, by routing a trench for the axle to sit in, or recess the ends of the fixing bolts.

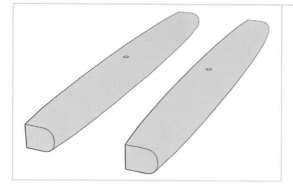

06 Now add more streamlined shaping to the axle supports. Note that we have only rounded over one side of them—the front-facing sides.

Use a plane and sandpaper to bring the surfaces to an even and smooth finish. This is worth the work, as they are an important feature of the cart.

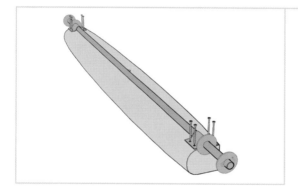

07 Practice setting up your wheels on the ends of the axle rod and on top of the axle support. Gauge the length of axle required including all washers and a stub extending each side—about 10 mm

(⅜ in) long—that can be drilled to take a split pin. Cut and drill the axle and file the ends very smooth. Do the same for the other axle. Fix both axles using brackets and screws so they do not turn.

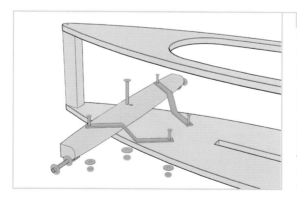

08 Fix the back axle in position using the bolts and the pre-drilled holes in the floor board. Make the suspension arms from stainless steel strap, following the template on page 85; the shape is not critical. Bend the metal in the vise using a hammer. Work gradually and protect the metal from the vise and hammer with small scraps

of wood. The suspension arms are first bolted loosely to the floor board, the axle is positioned in a perfectly square position (90° to the center line of the cart) and the suspension arms are swung into position. Mark the holes through the ends of the arms and on to the axle support. Drill and fix. Tighten all the bolts properly.

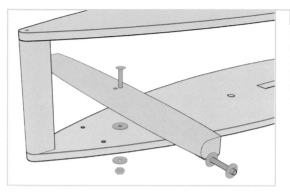

09 Now fix the pivoting front axle using the pre-drilled holes. Use washers where indicated to allow free movement and to spread the load.

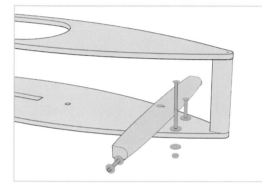

10 The two remaining holes at the front are for the steering limiters. These bolts stick up from the floor board and prevent the axle from pivoting too far and the wheels from snarling with the body shell. Some race rules specify the limitation of the steering, so check that out. We have used tube sleeves around the bolts to protect the axle support.

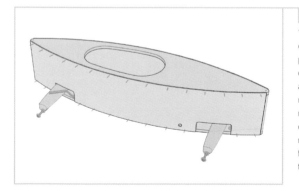

11 Cut out the sides of the cart using the template on page 85 as a guide. The shape of the arches around each axle is critical; we would recommend that you first make a full-size pattern from cardboard and test the fit. You must allow sufficient room for the front axle to turn and the back suspension arms to flex. Don't make the holes bigger than necessary. Include a hole for the steering cable. Fit the sides using glue and pins spaced at 100 mm (4 in) intervals. When dry, plane the edges flush with the top and bottom, knock the pin heads below the surface of the wood slightly, fill over the pin heads, and sand smooth.

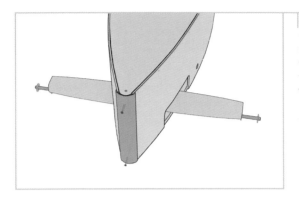

12 Finish off both ends using metal trim. We have used textured aluminum sheet, bent to suit the shape, and fixed with two screws.

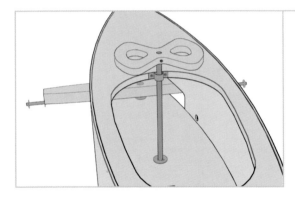

13 The steering column is a solid metal rod that is captured in the pre-drilled hole in the floor using a washer and split pin on either side, so it can pivot but not move up or down. Make or find a bracket to support the top of the steering coloumn and fix that with screws running into the thickness of the top board.

Make the steering wheel as shown on the template on page 85. Cut a small square of plywood to reinforce the underside of the steering wheel and provide more "meat "for around the column. Fix the steering wheel to the column using a screw or bolt as shown.

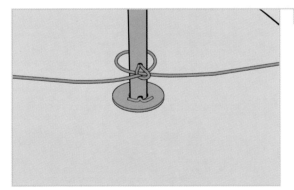

14 Drill a hole through the steering column running from front to back, with the steering wheel positioned how you want it. This diagram shows the bottom of the steering column inside the cart looking toward the front. Fold the cable in half and poke the halfway point loop through the hole toward you. Then,

one side at a time, pass the end of the cable back around the column and through the loop. Pull it up as tight as you can and the cable will stay in position. Now wrap each end of the cable all the way around the column at least once. Feed each end through the pre-drilled holes in the sides of the cart.

STEERING

One of the problems with cable steering is that the cable stretches a bit and you are forever retensioning it. For easier maintenance, you can include two tension bolts on each side of the cable either in the cart—better from a wind resistance point of view—or outside the cart, near to where the cable joins the axle support. The last option looks really cool and is easier to get at. If you want a cart with quicker, albeit heavier, steering, use a larger-diameter steering column.

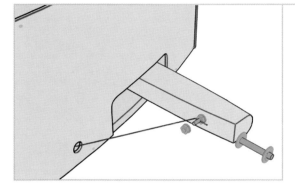

15 Connect the ends of the steering cable to the front axle support, somewhere not far from the ends. This distance should be equal on both sides. We have used bolts with holes drilled in the ends, through which a cable is passed and clamped by a nut—similar to how brake cables are sometimes fixed on bikes. Ask a friend to hold the steering wheel straight while you pull each cable tight and do up the nuts. Retension as required.

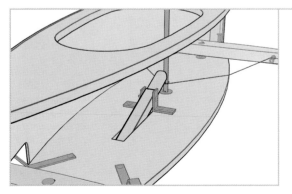

16 Find two right-angle brackets for fixing the brake lever to the floor or make your own brackets from stainless steel. Screw a block of rubber or folded piece of old bike tire to the end of the lever nearest the floor. Fit a spring near the brackets between the brake handle and the floor so the brake stays off until you pull the handle.

BRAKES

This cart uses a brake lever in the floor that acts on the ground. It could also be a vertical plunging variety if you prefer, which takes up far less room. These have more vibration problems, however, and have to be very heavily built. More efficient brake designs, such as linear or side-pull caliper brakes, can be mounted on the axle supports if your wheels have suitable rims; these can look really cool. Normally, brakes are not used at all during a race, although you must have them anyway.

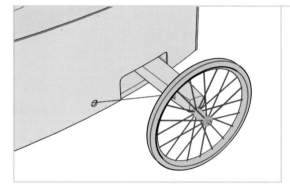

17 Fit the wheels on the axles. Finish with a washer and split pin through the pre-drilled holes. If the wheel has any movement along the axle, add another washer or two until it is tight. Test your cart. If you are happy, remove the wheels, and any metalwork you want to protect from paint, sand everything again with fine sandpaper, and apply the finish. Varnish the top first, let it dry, lightly sand, and then recoat. With the varnish dry, apply the paint, sanding lightly after the first coat. Allow several days to dry properly before reassembling.

WHEELS AND BEARINGS

It goes without saying, but wheels with bearings are a good idea if you are going to race; they are not so important otherwise. We have used wheels with roller bearings—they are a good fit on the axle and spin freely. If you are using a different type of wheel that has ball bearings and a stub axle, then fix that directly to the axle supports. If the stubs are very short, less than 100 mm (4 in), it is best to link the wheels by welding an axle in between. Bike wheels could be used by welding an axle to the spindles.

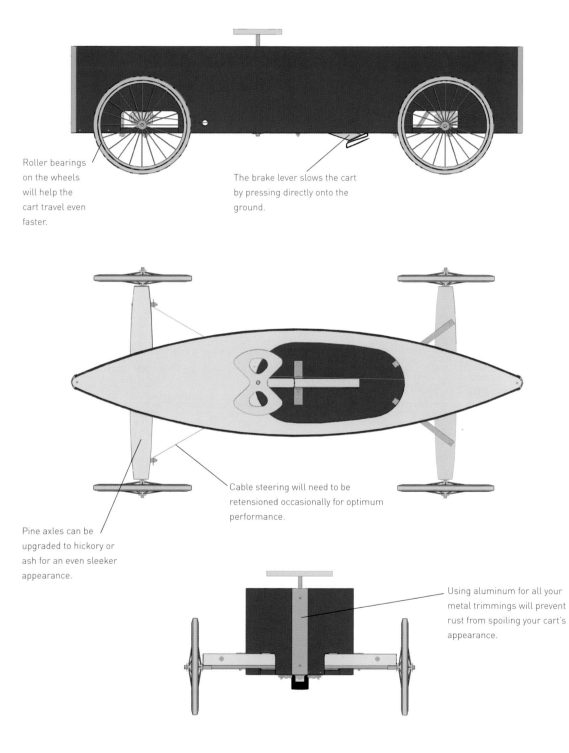

Roller bearings on the wheels will help the cart travel even faster.

The brake lever slows the cart by pressing directly onto the ground.

Cable steering will need to be retensioned occasionally for optimum performance.

Pine axles can be upgraded to hickory or ash for an even sleeker appearance.

Using aluminum for all your metal trimmings will prevent rust from spoiling your cart's appearance.

The Pedal-Powered Cart

THIS IS A SNAZZY CART FOR CHILDREN OF ALL AGES. Its streamlined design and chunky wheels make it fun to ride on grass and hard surfaces. The direct-chain drive means you also have reverse gear and don't need brakes. Supervise your child at all times and stay away from hills until the child is older.

YOU WILL NEED

Some basic tools:
- Useful tools are a tape measure
- Pencil
- Jigsaw
- Drill/driver with bits
- Hacksaw
- File
- Pliers
- Coarse sandpaper
- A workbench
- Vise

Some wood:
- You need a small amount of strong plywood. Find some good-quality pieces with a smooth knot-free surface (see pages 96–97 for sizes)
- Birch plywood is the best if you don't mind the high price tag. This will make life much easier when you are sanding and preparing to paint

Some metal:
- 10–12 mm (⅖–½ in) diameter solid steel axles are ideal and you can use the same section of material for the steering column and crank. These can be bought from a DIY store. That is about all you need apart from the usual nuts, bolts, and washers

You also need:
- Four chunky wheels that you can buy new or salvage from an old toy
- The same goes for the pedals, chain, and sprockets (wheels with teeth that mesh with the chain)
- The chain is from a bike with derailer gears; unravel it and it's surprisingly long! It is possible to modify the gear ratio by varying the diameter (and the tooth count) of the sprockets on each end of the chain
- For this cart, look around for similar-size sprockets and check that they mesh with the chain

The position of the seat is adjustable, so this is great for any child. The chain is mostly covered so is quite safe. This is a great opportunity for a decorative paint job; consider flames, stripes, stars, or spirals.

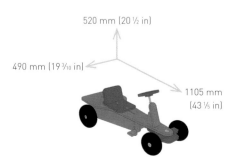

520 mm (20 ½ in)

490 mm (19 ³/₁₀ in)

1105 mm (43 ⅕ in)

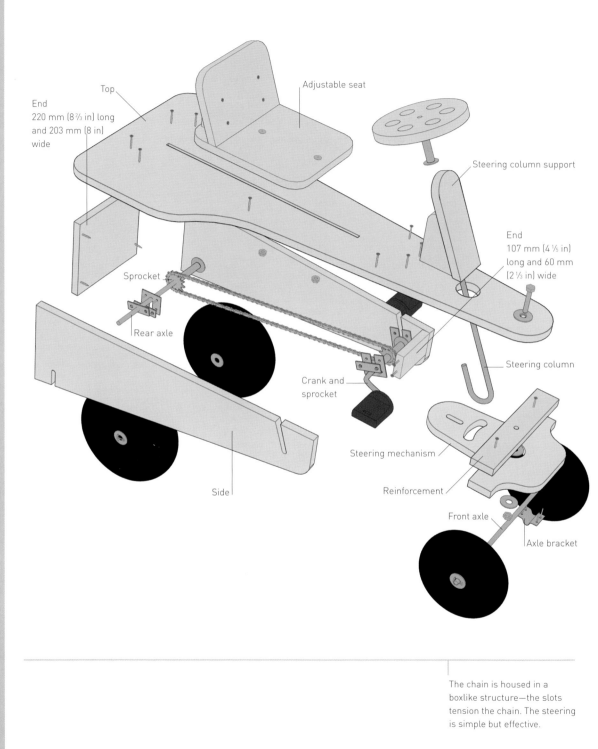

End
220 mm (8 ⅔ in) long
and 203 mm (8 in)
wide

Top

Adjustable seat

Steering column support

End
107 mm (4 ⅛ in)
long and 60 mm
(2 ⅓ in) wide

Sprocket

Rear axle

Steering column

Crank and
sprocket

Steering mechanism

Reinforcement

Side

Front axle

Axle bracket

The chain is housed in a
boxlike structure—the slots
tension the chain. The steering
is simple but effective.

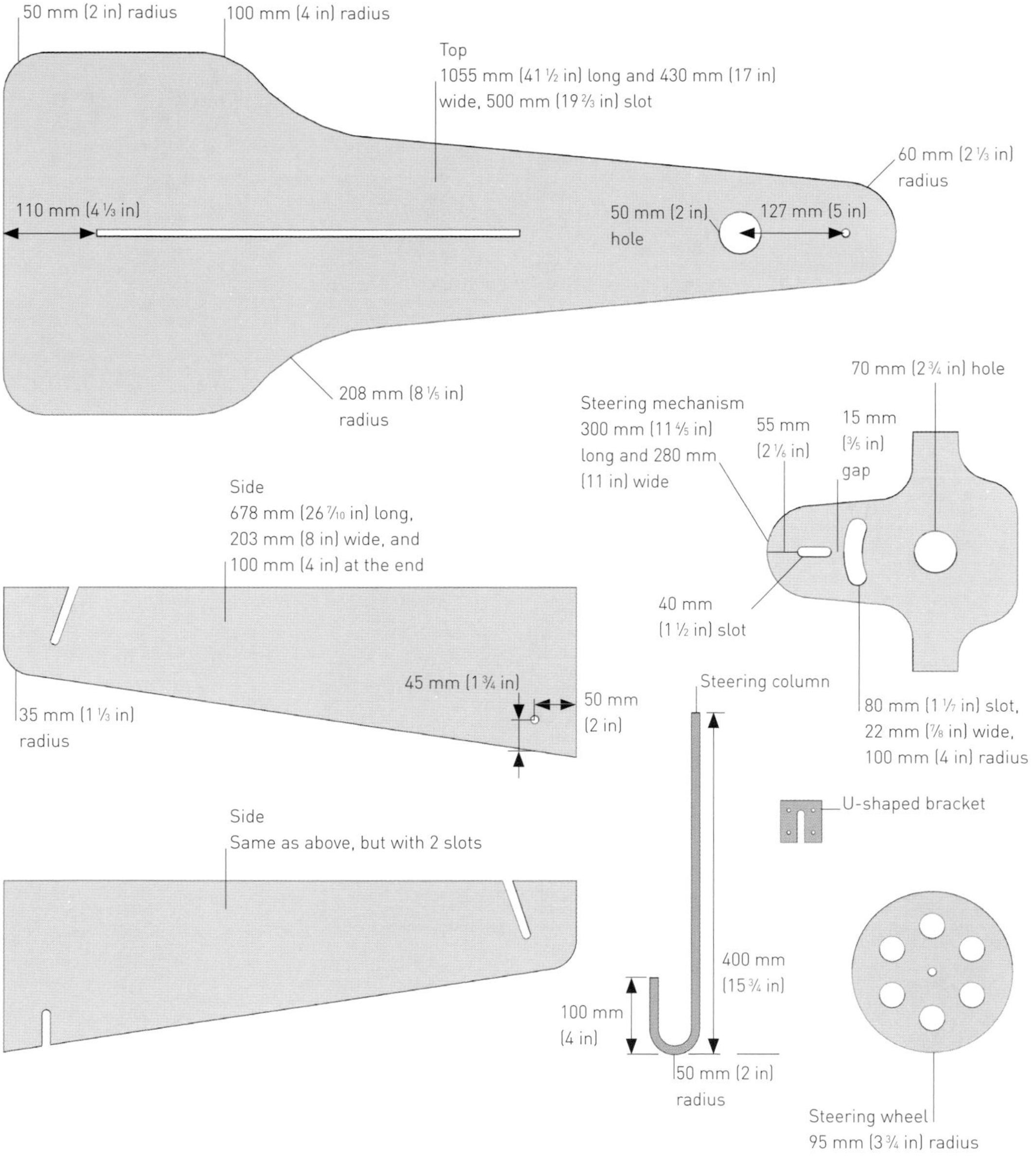
50 mm (2 in) radius
100 mm (4 in) radius
Top
1055 mm (41 ½ in) long and 430 mm (17 in) wide, 500 mm (19 ⅔ in) slot
60 mm (2 ⅓ in) radius
110 mm (4 ⅓ in)
50 mm (2 in) hole
127 mm (5 in)
208 mm (8 ⅕ in) radius
70 mm (2 ¾ in) hole
Steering mechanism
300 mm (11 ⅘ in) long and 280 mm (11 in) wide
55 mm (2 ⅙ in)
15 mm (⅗ in) gap
Side
678 mm (26 7/10 in) long, 203 mm (8 in) wide, and 100 mm (4 in) at the end
40 mm (1 ½ in) slot
45 mm (1 ¾ in)
Steering column
35 mm (1 ⅓ in) radius
50 mm (2 in)
80 mm (1 1/7 in) slot, 22 mm (⅞ in) wide, 100 mm (4 in) radius
U-shaped bracket
Side
Same as above, but with 2 slots
400 mm (15 ¾ in)
100 mm (4 in)
50 mm (2 in) radius
Steering wheel
95 mm (3 ¾ in) radius

Templates for the plywood shapes, steering column, and U bracket. The steering wheel and bracket might be features you can find ready-made.

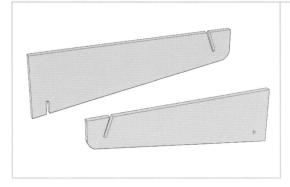

01 Mark out the two side-piece shapes on to the plywood using a tape measure, pencil, and compass (see template on page 97). The sides are identical so you can cut one and mark around it to get the other shape, but note that there is a difference in the slot and hole in the back corner. The slots are to allow for assembling and tensioning the chain; the axle and crank should slide up and down the slots. Sand the wood smooth and round over sharp corners and edges. Do that to all the plywood pieces in the cart.

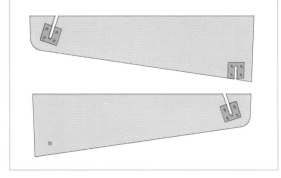

02 Make or buy some U-shaped metal brackets —again the axle and crank should slide within the slot. These are screwed to the inside faces of the sides as shown; their purpose is to reinforce the wood. Cut a piece of steel tube to fit in the remaining hole in the back corner of the cart and file the tube ends smooth. This lines and reinforces the hole. The axle should slide through the tube—the tube should be a tight enough fit to need a hammer to knock it in.

03 Make the ends of the box structure, drill holes for fixing with screws, and assemble. When you are satisfied with the fit, you need to remove one side—the nearest side in the diagram—to allow for fitting the axle, chain, and crank.

CHAIN ADJUSTMENT

The angled slots for the crank to slide down are intended for tensioning the chain. This design uses a chain from a pre-teen bike so it is not as long as that of an adult bike. Reducing the length of the chain is a very easy job if you have the tools (so it would be no trouble in a bike-repair shop), but it is probably easier to modify the position of the slot to suit your chain. Practice putting together your chain and sprockets, check that they work, and measure the distance between the sprocket centers.

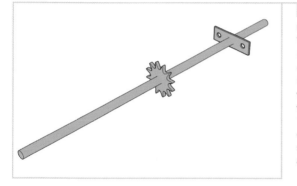

04 This shows the back axle. Work out the length of axle required. You should start overlength, position it in your box structure, thread on the wheels and all necessary washers, and allow for 10 mm (⅜ in) stubs extending out from the wheels either side. Cut the axle to length and round over the ends with a file. Make and weld a plate to the axle as shown. This is for fixing the axle to the inside face of the rear wheel. The holes should be suitably positioned for fixing near the center of the wheel in an appropriate way —screwed into a solid area, for example. Weld the sprocket to the center of the axle.

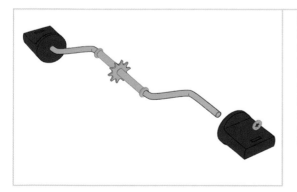

05 Make a crank to fit through the sides of the box structure. Thread the sprocket and weld in the center position and add the tube spacers and washers before you start bending the crank. The extent of the bends are not critical, but they need to be equal either side and the ends must be parallel with the center portion. Attach the pedals with starlock washer fixings (as shown) or bolts, depending on the design. You can make pedals from hardwood, but they would need to be quite chunky to withstand the rigors of use.

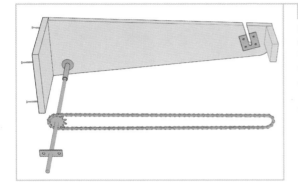

06 Assemble the back axle and chain in the box structure. Use a length of tube and a washer as a spacer to fix the axle in a central position. Replace the other side of the cart and tighten the screws.

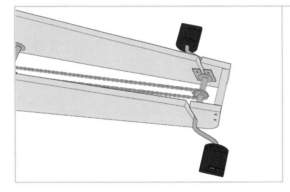

07 Engage the crank sprocket in the chain and slide the crank into the slots at the front. Push down to tighten the chain.

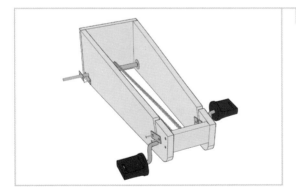

08 Buy plates of metal to fit under the back axle on one side and over the crank on both sides. Check the chain is tight, drill pilot holes through the plates, and fix with screws.

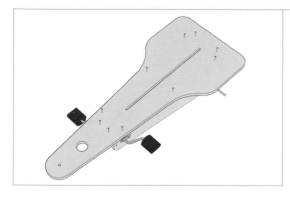

09 Make the top board using strong plywood. Follow the template on page 97. The shape can be marked out using a tape measure, pencil, compass, and straight edge. Cut the slot for the seat bolts with a jigsaw; drill a hole at each end of the slot and saw out in between. Use a holesaw for the large hole for the steering column and drill the front axle pivot hole. Fix the top board to the box structure using screws in the approximate locations shown.

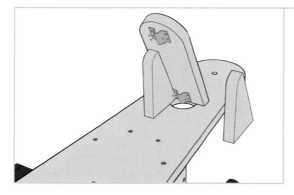

10 Cut the pieces of plywood for the steering column support and position over the hole so that the column runs through the hole in a central position. Fix to each other and to the top board using long screws driven into the thickness of the plywood at suitable angles. Fix two metal brackets to the plywood as shown. These should allow the column to turn freely.

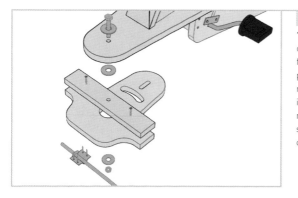

11 Mark out the shapes of the front axle supports following the template on page 97. The top piece is a reinforcing rectangle that is screwed to the top of the more complicated shape. This shape is critical, so mark and cut carefully. Work out the front axle length in the same way as you did for the back, and fix it to the underside of the support. Bolt the front axle assembly to the front of the cart. The nut and washer are housed in the recess created in the axle support.

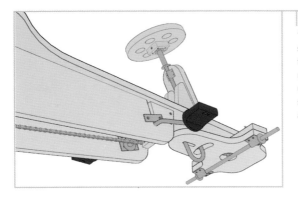

12 Make a steering wheel as shown by the template, or find a ready-made one. This requires a reinforcing block underneath as shown. Make a steering column with a crook at the end—this shape is critical—push that up through the cart as shown, add the spacer and washers at the top, and attach the steering wheel with a screw run through the reinforcing block.

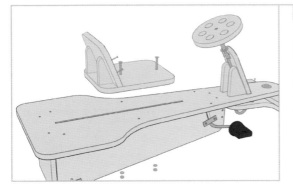

13 Make the seat using plywood and screws and use bolts to fit it to the slot in the cart. Check that the seat can move up and down properly, choose a suitable position, and tighten the bolt.

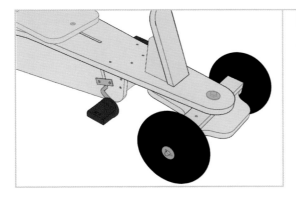

14 Attach the wheels using washers, with split pins inserted through holes in the ends of the axles, and test drive. If all is okay, remove the wheels and apply a paint finish. You may wish to remove or mask parts and paint them individual colors. When dry, reassemble. Oil the chain. The option remains to fit a rectangle of thin plywood to the underside to enclose the chain. This is recommended for younger children, who may not understand the dangers of playing with the chain.

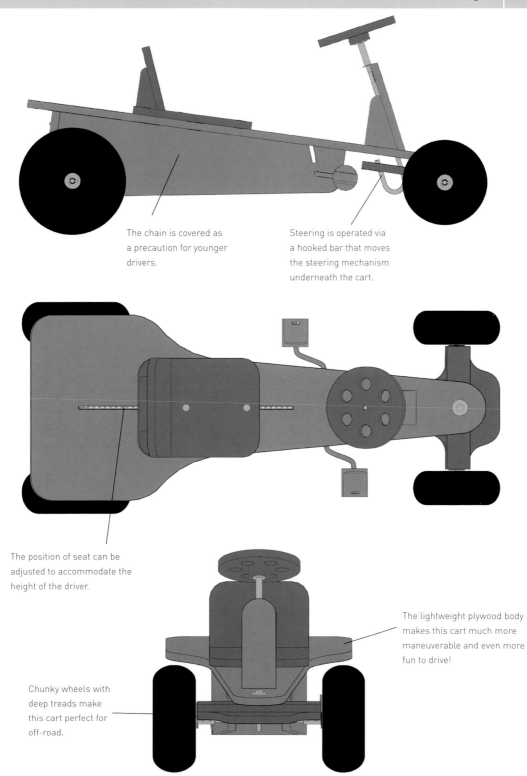

The chain is covered as a precaution for younger drivers.

Steering is operated via a hooked bar that moves the steering mechanism underneath the cart.

The position of seat can be adjusted to accommodate the height of the driver.

The lightweight plywood body makes this cart much more maneuverable and even more fun to drive!

Chunky wheels with deep treads make this cart perfect for off-road.

The Gasoline Go-Cart

THIS HANDBUILT GASOLINE GO-CART WILL GET YOU TO THE FINISH LINE FIRST! Actually it's not the fastest cart around, but it is very noisy and great fun. The engine is your starting point, but with a funky frame, robust steering geometry, and high-performance pneumatic tires there will be no stopping you!

YOU WILL NEED

Some basic tools:
- For this cart you need to decide how much of the tube bending and welding you want to do yourself. If you prefer, ask a metal fabricator to do the bulk of it. Budget-wise, it is obviously cheaper to build everything yourself, especially if you have the kit and welding skills. A MIG (metal inert gas) welder and a manual tube bender are ideal for this work
- You will also need the usual handtools for measuring, marking, cutting, and finishing, plus a set of wrenches or a socket set. You may need a pop riveter for fixing the floor plate, depending on the material you use

Some metal:
- Tube—if you buy it from a metal supplier—is cheap, which is good news as you need quite a bit. However, in the true spirit of soapbox cart building, you can make this cart from reclaimed steel tube!
- Old play equipment like a swing frame, for example, has great potential—use the bends to make your own unique frame design
- Even some quality strollers have thick, strong tubes. Avoid using feeble thin-walled stuff. Other small bits of sheet, plate, and equal-angle steel are needed, plus some sheet metal for the floor area, chain guard and steering column, which can be aluminum or steel
- You may need to get help with the back axle, which needs some machining

You also need:
- A suitable engine in good working order—we have used a Honda G150, 144 cm^3
- A clutch
- Sprockets
- A disk brake
- Wheels
- Plastic seat
- A steering wheel—ours is from a Mini

This cart has some great features, including a frame with a low center of gravity and versatile engine-mounting space. The pedal-operated throttle and disk brake gives kids a real driving experience. Kids must receive clear instructions and safety advice, wear a helmet, and be supervised at all times.

640 mm (25 ⅕ in)

830 mm (32 ⅔ in)

1600 mm (63 in)

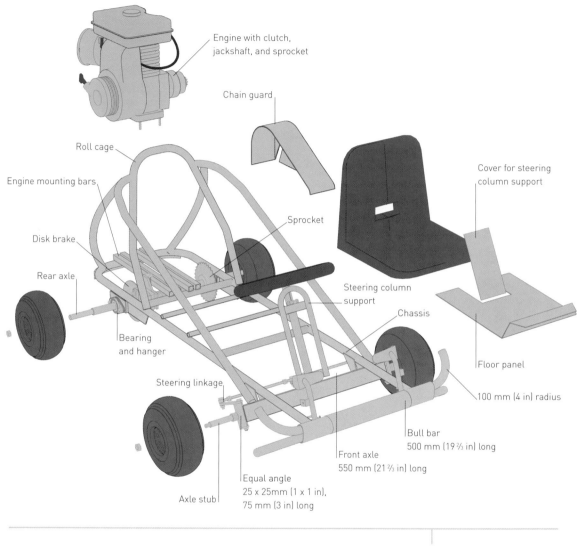

Engine with clutch, jackshaft, and sprocket

Chain guard

Roll cage

Engine mounting bars

Disk brake

Rear axle

Bearing and hanger

Sprocket

Steering column support

Chassis

Cover for steering column support

Floor panel

100 mm (4 in) radius

Bull bar
500 mm (19 ⅔ in) long

Steering linkage

Axle stub

Equal angle
25 x 25mm (1 x 1 in),
75 mm (3 in) long

Front axle
550 mm (21 ⅔ in) long

An exploded drawing giving a clear view of the complete frame before the wheels, engine, seat, and sheet metal parts are attached.

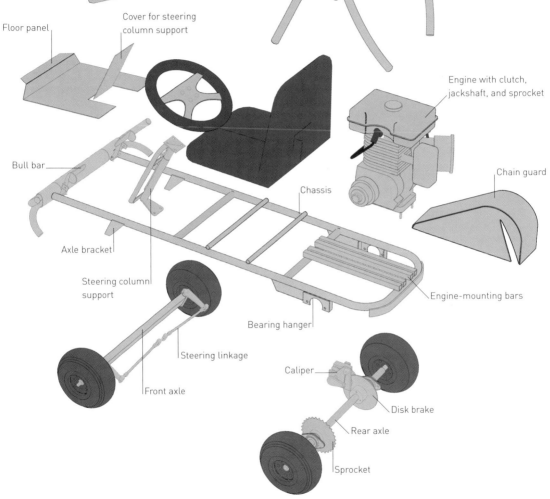

Roll cage

Cover for steering
column support

Floor panel

Engine with clutch,
jackshaft, and sprocket

Bull bar

Chain guard

Chassis

Axle bracket

Steering column
support

Engine-mounting bars

Bearing hanger

Steering linkage

Caliper

Disk brake

Rear axle

Front axle

Sprocket

An exploded rear view showing
the front axle and steering,
rear axle with sprocket,
disk brake, and the other
parts separated off from the
chassis.

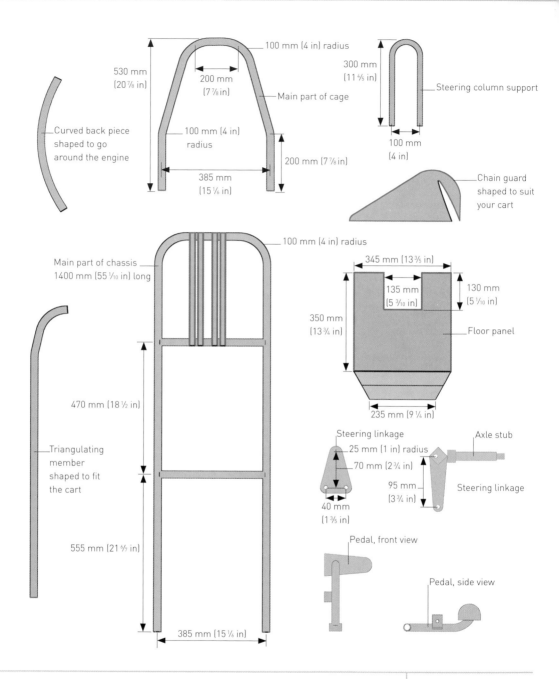

100 mm (4 in) radius

530 mm
(20 ⅞ in)

200 mm
(7 ⅞ in)

Main part of cage

Curved back piece
shaped to go
around the engine

100 mm (4 in)
radius

385 mm
(15 ⅛ in)

200 mm (7 ⅞ in)

300 mm
(11 ⅘ in)

Steering column support

100 mm
(4 in)

Chain guard
shaped to suit
your cart

100 mm (4 in) radius

Main part of chassis
1400 mm (55 ¹⁄₁₀ in) long

470 mm (18 ½ in)

Triangulating
member
shaped to fit
the cart

555 mm (21 ⁶⁄₇ in)

385 mm (15 ⅛ in)

345 mm (13 ⅗ in)

135 mm
(5 ³⁄₁₀ in)

130 mm
(5 ¹⁄₁₀ in)

350 mm
(13 ¾ in)

Floor panel

235 mm (9 ¼ in)

Steering linkage

25 mm (1 in) radius

70 mm (2 ¾ in)

40 mm
(1 ⅗ in)

95 mm
(3 ¾ in)

Axle stub

Steering linkage

Pedal, front view

Pedal, side view

Templates for producing the
chassis and other shaped
components: the cage, parts
of the steering mechanism,
the chain guard, the floor
panel, and the pedals.

TUBE BENDING

Tubing of this size can be bent using a manual tube bender, which you can get from a local machine supplier. The process is very simple but practice is needed before you can achieve consistent results. We have used the same radius for many parts, so that will make things easier. Test-bending using your machine should tell you where to start your bends—bending typically starts later than you think it will—so judging the distance between two bends as in step 1 below should not be too difficult.

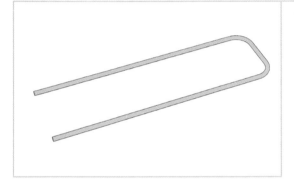

01 Use the tube bender to make the main part of the chassis (see template opposite). If the width comes out differently to what you expect then you may want to cut through the metal at the end and weld back together at the right size.

WELDING

We have used a MIG welder because it is quick and strong, but you can also used a TIG welder or gas welder. To weld successfully, you need to receive tuition from an expert welder. Eye protection must be worn at all times. Follow the manufacturer's instructions on how to use the equipment safely. Alternatively, ask a metal fabricator to weld for you or modify the design so all the parts are bolted together. Use welding clamps to hold pieces in position while you work. Tack pieces and check them before finishing the joins.

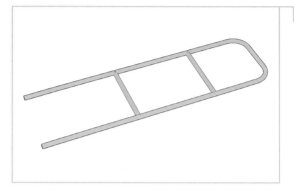

02 Cut and weld the intermediate struts in order to reinforce the chassis.

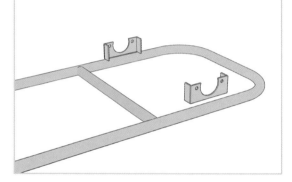

03 Make or buy some suitable bearing hangers. These will depend on the type of wheels, axle, and bearings you intend using, but these need to be very strong.

Use 3 mm (¹⁄₁₀ in)-thick steel and make a bent bracket shape for extra rigidity. Weld these in position to the underside of the chassis (shown here upside down).

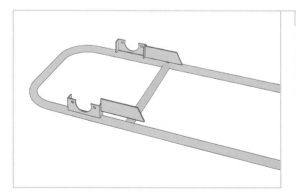

04 The area around the back axle is subject to the greatest forces, so reinforce the tubing using 3 mm (¹⁄₁₀ in)-thick steel plate as shown.

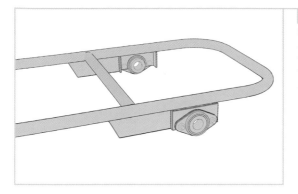

05 Test-fit the rear bearings as shown using bolts. Check the alignment by sliding the axle through; make adjustments if necessary.

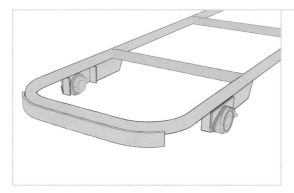

06 The weight of the engine when the cart is bouncing along may cause the tube to distort at the back unless you reinforce it. Weld a chunky band under the back of the frame.

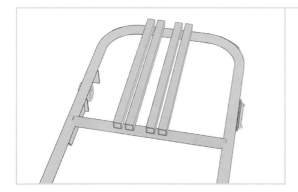

07 Work out the position of the engine mount crosspieces. These pieces of square-section thick-wall tubing provide slots for the engine to be bolted to. You need some adjustment of the engine position in the front-back direction in order to tension the chain. The position of these will vary according to your engine. The position is not critical at this stage since the sprocket on the axle can be aligned with the sprocket on the engine. However, you do need to test the position so the sprocket finishes in a convenient position within the area of the frame—see, for example, the position of the sprocket on the axle in the diagram on page 106.

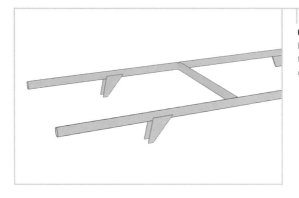

08 Cut and weld the front axle brackets either side of the tubing near the front of the cart. The front axle (see step 09) is welded to these at an angle equal to or close to the angle of the steering column.

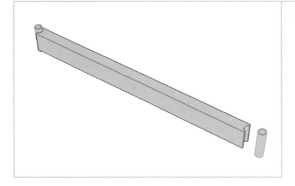

09 Make the front axle with tubes welded to the ends for attaching the pivoting stub axles. You can just weld them on square ends or, for a better joint, file a rounded shape in the end of the box section tubing.

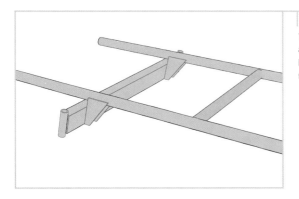

10 Weld the front axle in a central position to the brackets at the front of the cart.

BULL BAR

This feature is mainly about styling and makes the cart look more rugged, but it also helps absorb an impact if you are unlucky enough to crash into something, so I would recommend you include it. This one is a little elaborate, so you may want to simplify it to a single loop of tube or a large plate. Avoid sharp corners on the front of the cart, or for that matter anywhere on the cart.

11 Cut the large-diameter tube to length and mark positions 100 mm (4 in) in from the ends (shown here) to start squashing the ends to an oval shape. Use a vise to squash the tube and protect the metal from damage using scraps of wood either side. The finished oval shape should be suitable for receiving two pieces of bent tubing as in step 12.

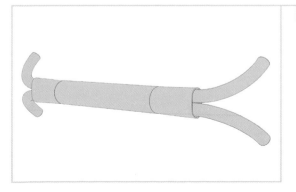

12 Bend four identical pieces of tubing for the ends of the bull bar and insert them into the larger tube as shown. The angle is not critical (see the side view on page 123). Weld the tubes together to form a rigid component. Cap the open ends.

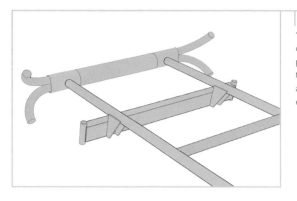

13 The bull bar completes the chassis. Weld it in a central position to the ends of the tubes—tack it in place first and check the angle of the ends.

14 Bend a piece of tubing for the main part of the cage and weld at an angle as shown in the side view on page 123. This angle is similar to the angle of the steering column.

15 Continue the cage construction, adding the long triangulating members to either side. Weld the lower ends to the top of the front axle. It helps to cut the ends to a corresponding angle before welding.

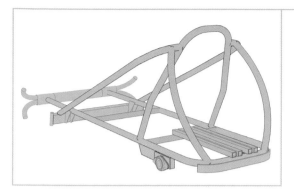

16 Complete the cage with curved pieces on either side at the back. Here, you may need to vary the shape as shown on the template on page 108.

They need to curve around the back of the engine; if yours is slightly bigger then you need more of a bend.

17 Make the steering column support using tube and plate bent and welded as shown. The steering column must fit within the tube welded to the plate, so check you can find pieces of suitably sized tubing before you proceed.

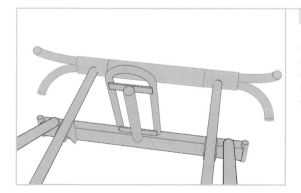

18 Weld the steering column support to the top of the front axle in a central position and at a suitable angle. See the side view on page 123 as a guide.

STEERING GEOMETRY

This cart uses straight steering linkages that are simple to make and effective. They are based on the Ackermann steering geometry—a method of steering designed to address the problem of wheels either side of a cart needing to follow different radii when cornering. You can improve this cart by fine-tuning the angle of the steering linkage in relation to the axle stub. Ideally, the pivot holes in the linkage should be in line with the centerpoint of the rear axle.

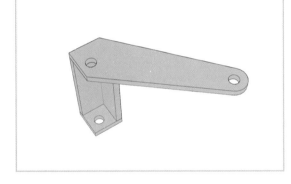

19 Make the steering linkage using a piece of equal-angle steel and some plate steel. Here the right-hand side is shown—don't make two identical ones!

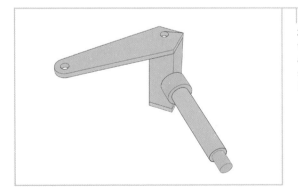

20 Weld the front axle stubs to the steering linkage in a central position and at a suitable angle. The right side is shown here.

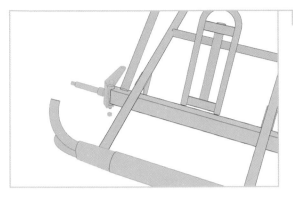

21 Attach the steering linkages to the ends of the front axle using bolts, nuts, and washers so that they pivot freely. Extra washers can be used to pack out the join and eliminate any up and down movement if the joint is loose.

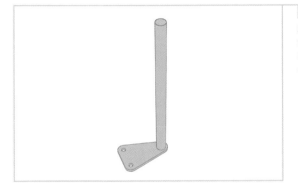

22 Weld the steering column to the linkage plate. The linkage plate needs to have rounded corners, as shown.

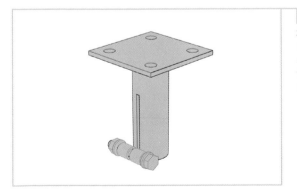

23 Make a steering wheel mount from tube and plate as shown. The size of the plate on top and the holes in it need to relate to your steering wheel. The slot in the tube allows the tube to flex and clamp around the steering column, thus preventing the column from slipping downward.

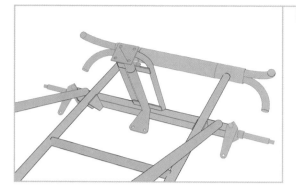

24 Pass the column up through the steering column support and clamp the steering wheel mount on top. The steering wheel mount and column should turn freely and not move up and down.

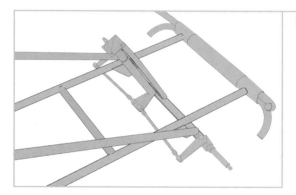

25 Connect the steering linkage to the base of the steering column using tie rods and rod ends (rose joints). These can be bought for the purpose and are fully adjustable. Set them so the axles stubs are at 90° to the cart frame and the column is in a straight position.

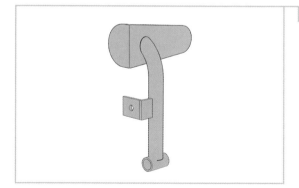

26 Make the pedals as shown, but don't forget they are a mirror image of each other— don't make two identical ones! Weld the tube and plate together. If you prefer, you can buy ready-made pedals.

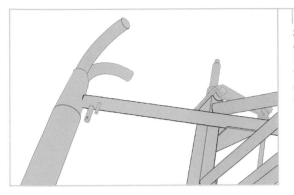

27 Weld a pivot pin—the larger of the two pins shown here— in the corner of the frame at the front for the pedals. Weld a smaller pin near to it as a stop to prevent the pedal from rotating further than required.

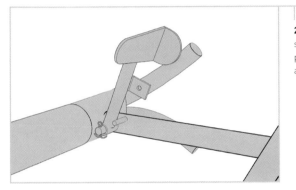

28 Attach the pedals to either side of the cart, check they pivot freely, and fix them with a split pin.

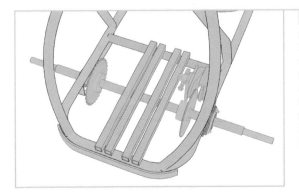

29 Onto the axle you need to locate the sprocket and the disk brake as shown using woodruff keys located in the slot milled into the axle. Fit the back axle in the bearings and bolt the assembly to the frame. Disk-brake design will vary quite a bit, so you will need to work out the best way of mounting the brake near to the disk by moving the disk along the axle to a suitable position. Weld a bracket to the frame to attach the brake to. Position the sprocket in alignment with the sprocket on your engine.

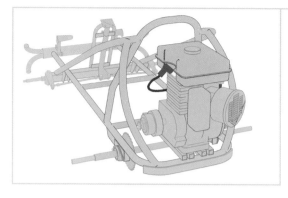

30 Now for the fun bit! Carefully—with the help of a friend—lift the engine in position and fix in the approximate location using bolts, nuts, and plate washers (large square washers). The bolts go through the slots in the square-section tubes. The sprockets should be aligned. Connect the chain over the sprockets. Adjust the engine position to tighten the chain. DANGER: DO NOT START THE ENGINE UNTIL THE CART IS COMPLETE. The exposed chain can cause serious injury if the engine is started.

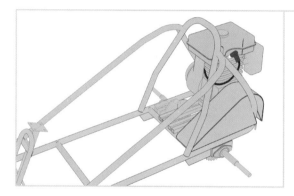

31 Make a chain guard from sheet metal—see the template on page 108 for a guide. Engine size varies, so you need to modify the shape to suit your engine. The idea is to cover up the moving parts as much as possible. We have used aluminum sheet, but steel is just as good. Weld tabs to the frame and bolt in position. You may need to cut a slot in the guard to fit around the cage.

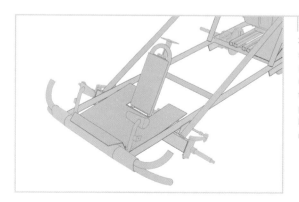

32 Make a floor plate and a steering-column plate from metal sheet—again we have used aluminum. Weld tabs to the cart frame and bolt in position. These do not have to be removed, so can be pop-riveted instead.

ADDITIONAL GUARD

We have not made a guard to go around the disk brake, but this is a good idea and recommended if the cart is going to be used by children. The spinning disk is less of a hazard than the chain, but it is better to be safe than sorry. Make this guard from sheet metal in a similar way to the chain guard. Of course, there are many parts of the cart that are a hazard—parts of the engine get very hot, for example—so you must explain the potential dangers to children.

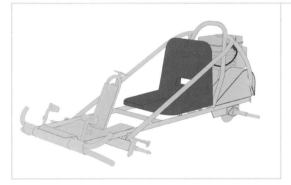

33 Fix a plastic seat in position. If you are using an old chair seat on a metal frame then you can probably detach the seat, cut off the legs, and weld the top bit of the frame to the cart and reattach the seat as before.

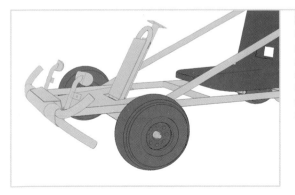

34 Bolt the wheels to the ends of the axles. The front non-drive wheels need bearings and the back ones do not; they locate on the axle with woodruff keys in a similar way to the disk brake and sprocket.

35 Attach the steering wheel using bolts. You can buy special competition butterfly steering wheels if you prefer. Link the disk brake to the brake pedal with cable, adjust, and tie securely to the frame at convenient locations. Attach the throttle cable to the throttle on the engine and the throttle pedal. Fit an engine cutoff switch to the frame somewhere within reach. See below on starting the cart. After testing, apply a paint finish—remove parts as necessary and reassemble when the paint is dry.

STARTING THE CART

Check that the chain is tight and the sprockets are aligned. Check the chain guard is in position. Prop up the cart so that the back wheels aren't touching the ground and chock the front wheels so the cart cannot move. Add fuel to the tank, turn on the fuel tap, and pull-start the engine. If the wheels do not start turning, throttle the engine until the clutch engages. Test that the engine cutoff switch works. Now you are ready for a test drive! Wear a helmet at all times and stay off public roads.

FINE-TUNING THE CART

Most small carts use Honda engines; these are very reliable, but, if like us you buy a used motor, you may have to tinker with it to get it running nicely! Take out the sparkplug and lay it on the engine while pulling the cord; you should see a healthy spark. If there is no spark then change the plug. If there is still no spark then you need a new ignition unit. Strip the carb and airline it out very carefully. Then clean out the fuel tank. The pilot jet screw needs to be about 1.5 turns out from seated. Set the idle screw for a smooth, slow tickover with no clutch drag. Don't forget to change the oil!

A low center of gravity equips the go-cart with excellent handling.

The Honda G150, 144 cm^3 engine combines performance with reliability.

The alignment of the steering linkages can be adjusted to increase the cart's performance on corners.

The chunky car steering wheel provides more grip and enhances the racing feel of the go-cart.

Using aluminum sheet for the foot rest helps to reduce the weight of the cart and therefore increase its performance.

The steel roll cage is durable and will protect the driver should the go-cart flip onto its side.

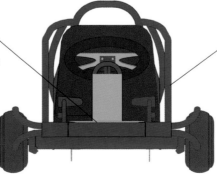

The Electric Go-Cart

THIS IS GREAT FUN FOR THE KIDS AND NICE AND QUIET FOR EVERYONE ELSE. No noisy engine this time, just a small electric motor and micro controller. Is it a go-cart or more of a back-to-front trike? Either way, it looks funky, it is easy to make, and does not have to cost the Earth.

YOU WILL NEED

Some basic tools:
- Hacksaw
- File
- A MIG, TIG, gas, or arc welder
- A metalwork vise mounted on a workbench is essential, especially when it comes to bending bits of metal
- A cordless drill/driver and bits
- Wrenches
- Tape measure
- Pliers

Some metal:
- Steel tube for the front axle
- Steel sheet for the battery and motor trays
- Some rectangular-section steel bar for the chassis. This can be purchased from a metal supplier; or you could use an old electric scooter

You also need:
- Three pneumatic wheels —one for fixing to an axle at the back with a suitable sprocket, and two buggy wheels with bearings and stub axles for the front and back axle
- A micro controller, Hall-effect throttle switch, and two batteries all need to have the same voltage rating of 12 V or 24 V
- Handlebar grips
- A plastic or metal box for the back
- A plastic seat from a chair

A three-wheeled variable-speed electric cart made from old bits of bike, scooter, plastic chair, stroller wheels, motor, and Hall-effect throttle switch. Don't be put off by the complicated-looking suspension arms—you can buy or reclaim ready-made suspension, or do without it.

555 mm (21 ⅞ in)

915 mm (36 in)

1290 mm (50 ⅘ in)

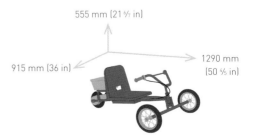

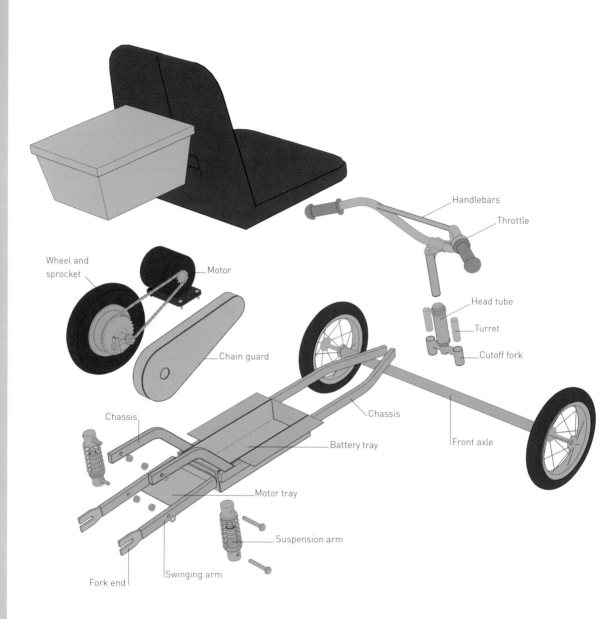

Labels: Handlebars, Throttle, Wheel and sprocket, Motor, Head tube, Turret, Cutoff fork, Chain guard, Chassis, Chassis, Front axle, Battery tray, Motor tray, Suspension arm, Swinging arm, Fork end

Exploded diagram revealing the construction of the chassis and rear suspension. Optional brakes, batteries, and cable are not shown.

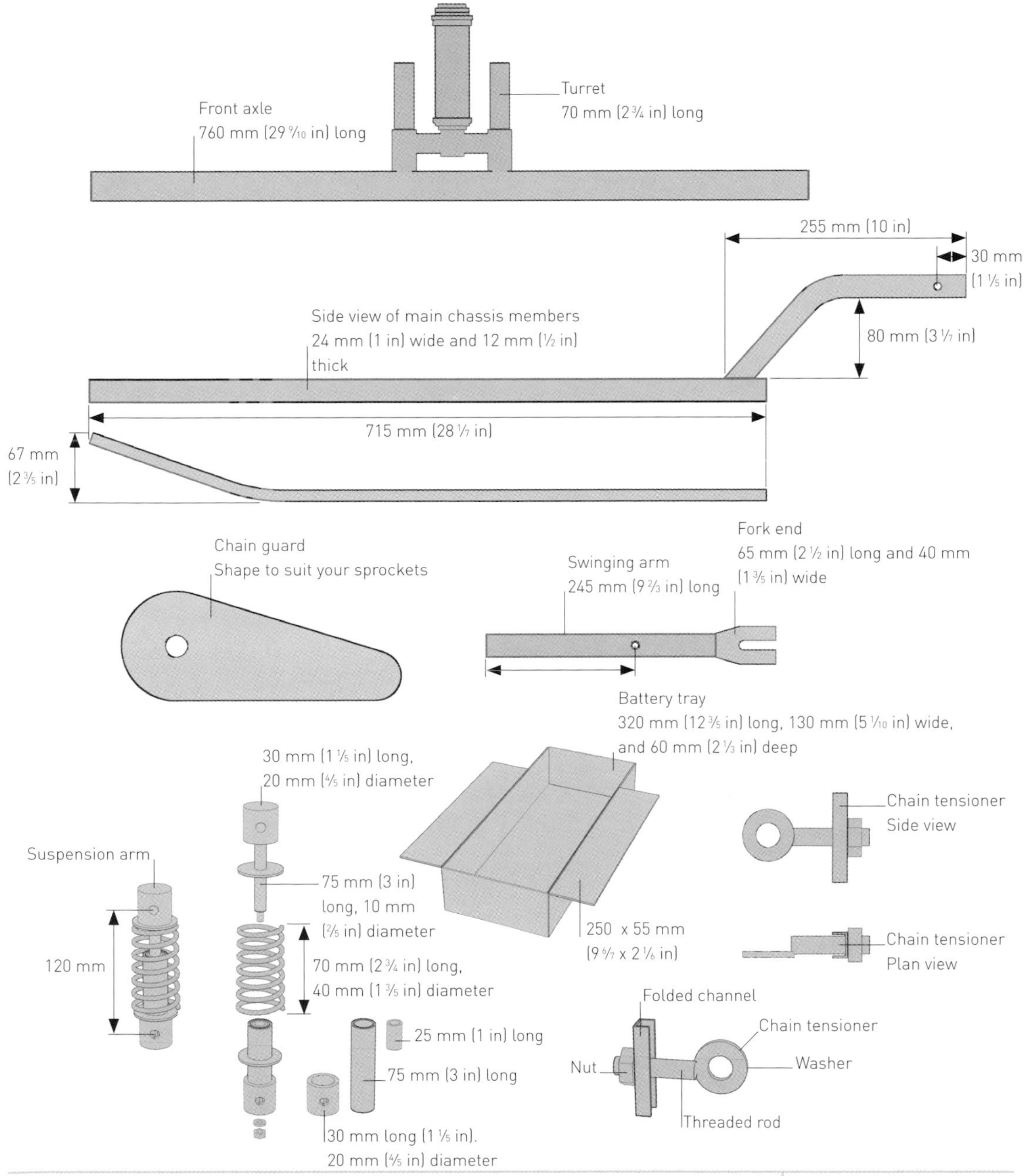
Front axle
760 mm (29 9/10 in) long
Turret
70 mm (2 3/4 in) long
255 mm (10 in)
30 mm
(1 1/5 in)
Side view of main chassis members
24 mm (1 in) wide and 12 mm (1/2 in)
thick
80 mm (3 1/7 in)
715 mm (28 1/7 in)
67 mm
(2 3/5 in)
Chain guard
Shape to suit your sprockets
Swinging arm
245 mm (9 2/3 in) long
Fork end
65 mm (2 1/2 in) long and 40 mm
(1 3/5 in) wide
Battery tray
320 mm (12 3/5 in) long, 130 mm (5 1/10 in) wide,
and 60 mm (2 1/3 in) deep
30 mm (1 1/5 in) long,
20 mm (4/5 in) diameter
Chain tensioner
Side view
Suspension arm
75 mm (3 in)
long, 10 mm
(2/5 in) diameter
120 mm
250 x 55 mm
(9 6/7 x 2 1/6 in)
Chain tensioner
Plan view
70 mm (2 3/4 in) long,
40 mm (1 3/5 in) diameter
Folded channel
Chain tensioner
25 mm (1 in) long
Nut
Washer
75 mm (3 in) long
Threaded rod
30 mm long (1 1/5 in).
20 mm (4/5 in) diameter

Templates and details necessary for constructing the cart. The suspension is discussed in more detail on page 132.

BUILD OR FIND

Components in this design can easily be substituted for found items—you do not have to build everything from scratch. Also, found items that are of slightly different design or size are probably going to be easy to accommodate in this design because it is so simple. The rear suspension is a good example of a component you might easily find ready-made. The motor, chain, and sprockets can also be reclaimed parts, but you need to check that they are compatible.

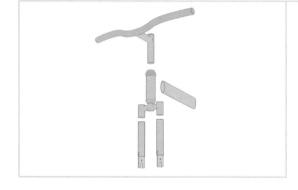

01 This cart uses the head tube from a children's bike (six to eight years) and the cow-horn handlebars from a children's scooter. Remove the ordinary handlebars, cut off the down tube—and top tube if it has one—flush with the head tube and file smooth. Cut off the forks as shown here and on the diagram on page 127. File the sharp edges smooth.

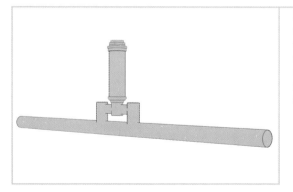

02 Prepare a front axle from steel tube and weld it in a central position to the underside of the forks. As with all welded joints, grind them smooth afterward.

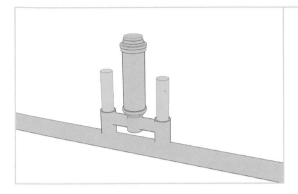

03 Weld two turrets on top of the forks. These will act as steering limiters and stop the front axle from pivoting too far and the cart falling over.

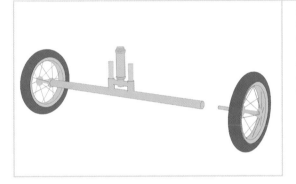

04 Find wheels with axle stubs —these can be from a good-quality but broken buggy—and weld them to the ends of the axle. The stubs do not have to fill the ends of the axle tube; they can be welded to the top surface through two holes in the tube or you can plug the ends of the axles and weld onto them. Bike wheels can also be used.

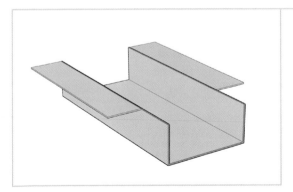

05 Make a battery tray from sheet steel. This needs to fit inside the frame (see exploded drawing on page 126) and also to accommodate two small 12v or 6 V batteries. Check the size of your batteries first! They can stick up a bit under the chair. This tray can be welded at all corners or made by bending the sheet using a vise, scrap wood to protect the metal, and a big hammer.

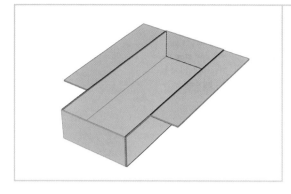

06 Now weld ends on to the battery tray. File or grind the joints to make them smooth.

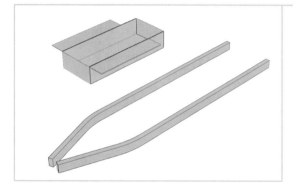

07 Make the sides of the chassis from rectangular-section solid steel. The template on page 127 shows the shape required. Hold the metal in a vise and simply pull on the long end and it will easily bend to shape. Make a matching pair and check that the tray fits between.

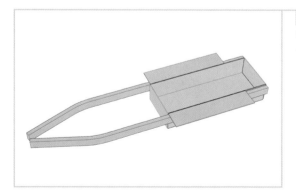

08 Weld the tray to the sides of the chassis so it lines up nicely.

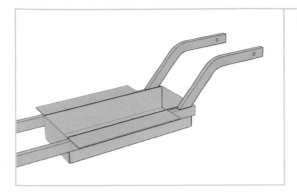

09 Make two more bent pieces from solid rectangular-section steel as shown on the template on page 127. This time the steel is bent across the width, which is difficult to do cold. It is much better to use a oxyacetylene or MAP gas torch to heat up the metal before bending it. Wear thick leather-welding gloves, an apron, and boots, and hold the metal in a vise while you work. Drill holes for the suspension arms to attach. Cut angled ends and weld them to the ends of the chassis.

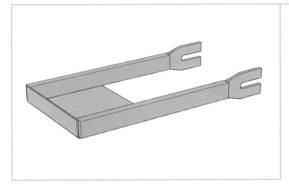

10 Make the swinging arm fork ends from thick steel plate and weld to more solid rectangular-section bar. Weld a sheet-steel end and bottom —for mounting the motor—to the frame. The sheet should overlap the frame so you can weld along the centerline. This is not critical, but does make a stronger joint.

MOTOR SIZE

Check that your motor fits the frame. If it is too long then it might stop the suspension from working. When the sides of the frame at the back (shown in step 9) are forced downward they should have room to move either side of the motor (see step 15). If there is not room, try to get a smaller motor or make a deep tray for the motor in step 10.

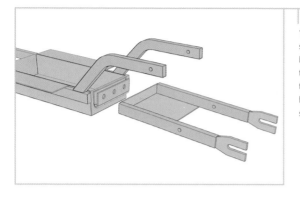

11 Find a really big, strong steel hinge and weld it to the back of the chassis as shown, then weld the back end of the frame to that. It should hinge freely, ready for the suspension arms to attach.

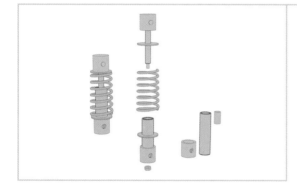

12 We recommend buying two moped gas suspension struts, but you could make a rough equivalent as follows. Full dimensions are given on page 127. Start by making the top part first from solid bar. A rod with a shoulder turned on the end is welded to that. The end is threaded to take a small washer and nut; this will stop the top coming apart from the bottom part. The large washers remain loose. The bottom half is made from three pieces of tube that slide inside each other—shown separately on the right of the diagram. The smallest piece of tube stops the top half from pulling out. Weld or braze the parts together. Assemble by compressing the ends against the spring and fitting the washer and nylon-insert locking nut.

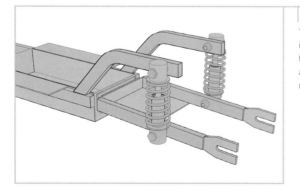

13 Bolt the suspension arms in position. Use three washers for each junction so that the arm can pivot freely. Use nylon-insert locking nuts.

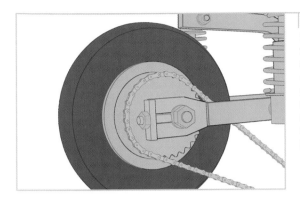

14 Mount the back wheel on the back axle along with the sprocket and chain. The wheel must be firmly fixed to the sprocket and turn freely on the axle. Ideally, the axle will have shoulders that fit between the forks and be threaded at the ends. Push the wheel and axle into the slots and into the forks. Make the chain-tension devices (shown in detail on page 127). Put the washer part over the ends of the axle and fit the end cap and nut. Do not tighten the nuts until the next step.

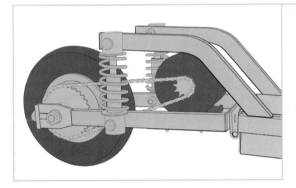

15 Fit the motor to the plate using nuts and bolts. The sprocket on the axle must align perfectly with the sprocket on the motor. Now use the chain tensioners to tighten the chain, but do not overdo it and stretch the chain —you just want to eliminate the slack. Tighten the nuts to secure the axle. DO NOT TEST THE MOTOR UNTIL THE CHAIN GUARD IS FITTED! Move the back wheel to check it turns without wobbling or becoming obstructed. Check that the chain is engaged properly. Now take out the back wheel and fit a chain guard, as shown below.

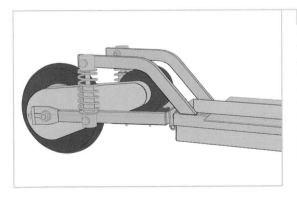

16 Make a chain guard to fit around the chain and sprockets. See the template on page 127 for an approximate guide to the shape. The actual shape will depend on your motor, chain, and sprocket. The shape should be about 20 mm (⅘ in) larger than the chain all around. The thickness of the guard should cover as much as possible, but leave about 25 mm (1 in) between the guard and the wheel. Fix the guard to the side of the bottom frame. Reattach the wheel, tension the chain, and check as before.

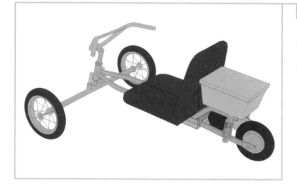

17 Weld the chassis to the front axle. Fit the handlebars, seat, and box at the back. Bolt the handlebars in place and adjust them. The plastic seat can be any type you like; it can be bolted or screwed from underneath into existing lugs. The box can be found or made and bolted to the frame from inside.

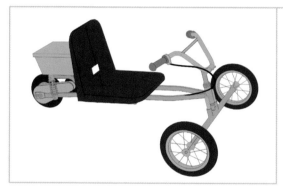

18 Fit the Hall-effect throttle switch and handlebar grips to the handlebars and connect the throttle to the motor via a micro controller. These items are available from suppliers on the internet or you may find them on old broken electric scooters or toys. Put the batteries in the tray under the seat and connect them to the micro controller. The batteries should be held down firmly with straps. The cart is self-braking to an extent, but you can fit disk or drum brakes. Test the bike. Paint as you like, but remove batteries prior to painting and disassemble parts that you want to protect from painting. Reassemble and enjoy, but be sure to keep off public footpaths and highways.

WIRING AND CHARGING

There are several common makes of micro controller. Buy the motor, controller, throttle, and charger from the same place to be certain they are compatible. The best systems are 24 V. For batteries, sealed lead-acid gel batteries are a must. Put a fuse and inline switch between the "+" from the batteries and the controller, and make sure the fuse is correct. For example, with a 10-amp motor use a 15-amp fuse. When you buy the equipment get an electrical schematic from the supplier and follow it carefully, making sure the drive wheel of the cart is not on the ground. Lastly, put in the fuse to test-run the cart.

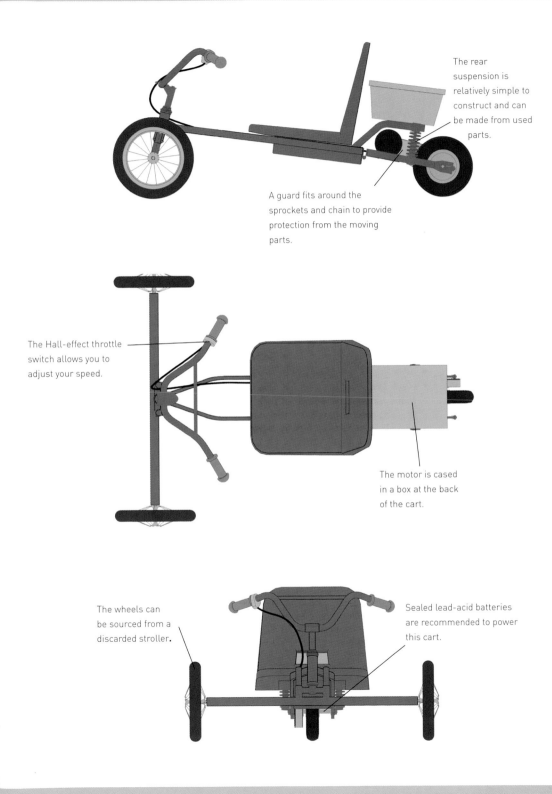

The rear suspension is relatively simple to construct and can be made from used parts.

A guard fits around the sprockets and chain to provide protection from the moving parts.

The Hall-effect throttle switch allows you to adjust your speed.

The motor is cased in a box at the back of the cart.

The wheels can be sourced from a discarded stroller.

Sealed lead-acid batteries are recommended to power this cart.

The Wind-Powered Cart

STRICTLY SPEAKING, THIS SHOULD PROBABLY
BE CALLED A LAND-YACHT. However, we think
this qualifies as a go-cart, and it's certainly one
for adrenaline junkies. It might seem crazy to the
uninitiated, but this concept has been around since
the pyramids were built, and became really popular
in the 1950s. You must wear a helmet and stay out of
strong winds.

YOU WILL NEED

Some basic tools:
- Tape measure
- Fine permanent
  marker pen
- Hacksaw
- File
- Metalwork vise
  mounted on a bench
- Jigsaw with a metal-
  cutting blade is
  ideal for cutting the
  aluminum sheet
- Big hammer and block
  of wood to squash the
  tube ends flat

- Pliers
- Knife
- If you are going to
  make the sail yourself
  you will need a sewing
  machine, chalk for
  marking out, and
  scissors

Some metal:
- Various sections of
  steel tube
- Two pieces of
  aluminum sheet for
  the seat
- Nuts

- Bolts
- Washers
- Pop rivets

Some professionally built
designs use aluminum
tube; this is better
because it is lighter, but
also costs a fortune (you
also need thicker section
tubes). Consider using it
only after trying out this
economy version.

You also need:
- The front part of a
  discarded kid's bike
- Two wheels (one big
  and one small)
- Fabric
- Sewing thread
- A sail eyelet
- Pullies
- A cleat
- Cord

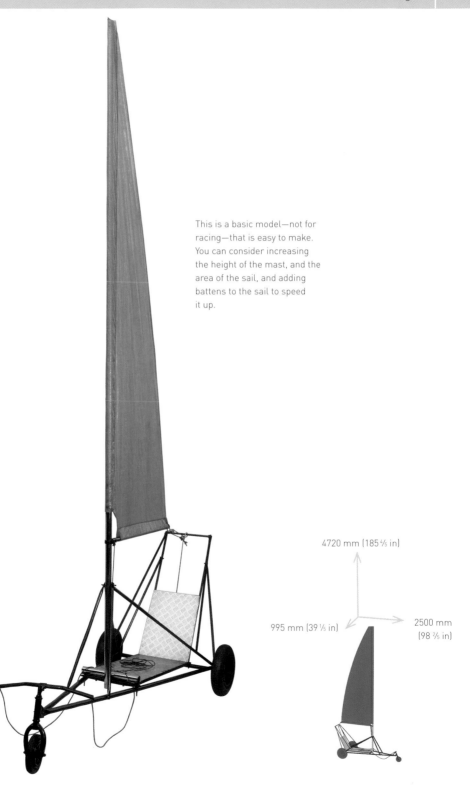

This is a basic model—not for racing—that is easy to make. You can consider increasing the height of the mast, and the area of the sail, and adding battens to the sail to speed it up.

4720 mm (185 ⅘ in)

995 mm (39 ⅛ in)

2500 mm (98 ⅖ in)

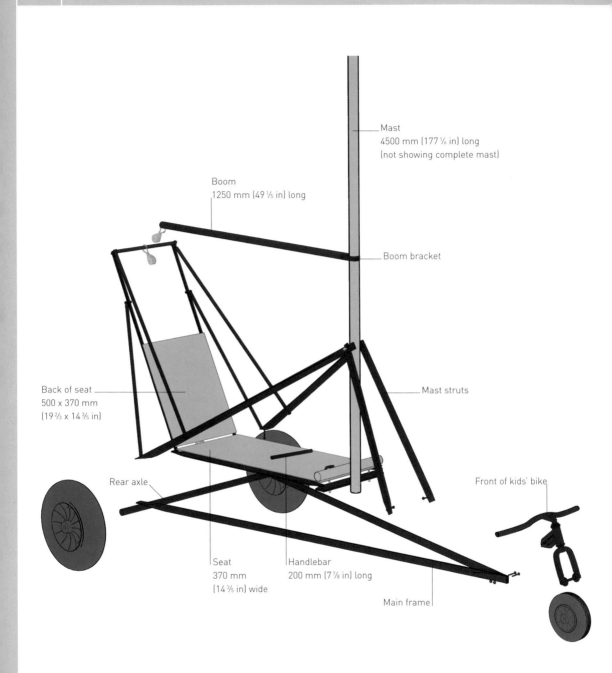

Mast
4500 mm (177 ⅙ in) long
(not showing complete mast)

Boom
1250 mm (49 ⅕ in) long

Boom bracket

Back of seat
500 x 370 mm
(19 ⅔ x 14 ⅗ in)

Mast struts

Rear axle

Front of kids' bike

Seat
370 mm
(14 ⅗ in) wide

Handlebar
200 mm (7 ⅞ in) long

Main frame

The strong triangulated
structure is made from
lengths of steel tube, mostly
with flattened and drilled
ends, all bolted together.

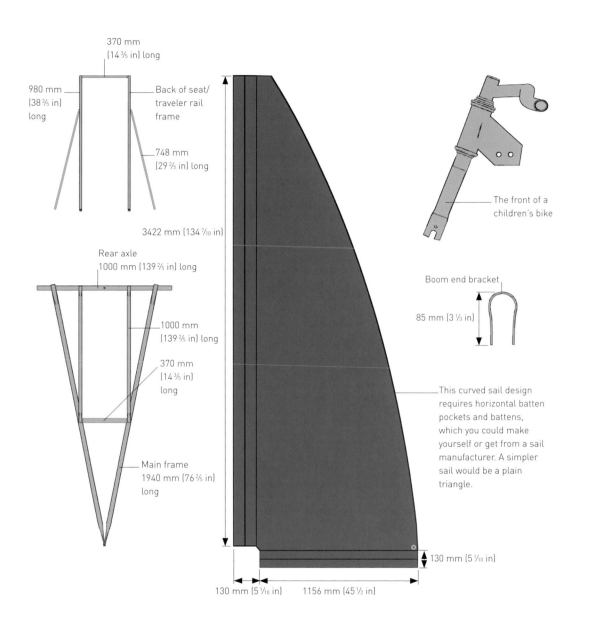

370 mm
(14 ³/₅ in) long

980 mm
(38 ³/₅ in)
long

Back of seat/
traveler rail
frame

748 mm
(29 ²/₅ in) long

3422 mm (134 ⁷/₁₀ in)

Rear axle
1000 mm (139 ²/₅ in) long

1000 mm
(139 ²/₅ in) long

370 mm
(14 ³/₅ in)
long

Main frame
1940 mm (76 ²/₅ in)
long

The front of a
children's bike

Boom end bracket

85 mm (3 ⅓ in)

This curved sail design
requires horizontal batten
pockets and battens,
which you could make
yourself or get from a sail
manufacturer. A simpler
sail would be a plain
triangle.

130 mm (5 ¹/₁₀ in)

130 mm (5 ¹/₁₀ in)   1156 mm (45 ½ in)

Here are the two main steel
frames, the pattern for the
sail, the portion of bike,
and the shape of the boom
bracket.

01 Look around for a broken, worn-out, or discarded children's bike—a five-year-old's bike is most suitable. Use the wheel from the bike or find another wheel that fits. This one had a single large oval-section down tube coming from the head tube, which is ideal. Cut through the tube frame at the point indicated (see template on page 138). The angle is not critical, but you may want to check if it's going to catch the end of your tubes before you cut. Other frame designs can also be used; use the top tube only and leave at least 150 mm (6 in) of tube for a good joint.

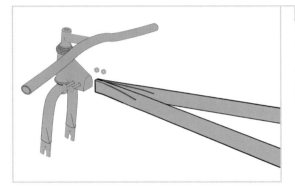

02 Cut two lengths of tube for the main frame—always file the ends smooth immediately after cutting them. Flatten about 100 mm (4 in) of the front ends and wedge into the bike frame. Drill and bolt in two places. For this project you don't need washers (although you can use them if you like), but you do need nylon-insert locking nuts.

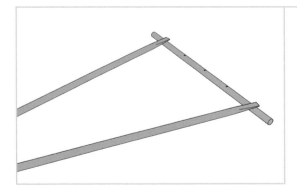

03 For the back end of the main frame, prepare an axle tube with five holes. Your back wheels must fit onto the ends of this axle, so work out how they are going to attach and adjust the dimensions of the axle accordingly. Our back wheels use roller bearings and fit over the axle, which is held on with washers and split pins. You can also use wheels with stub axles, or bike wheels with stubs welded on. Flatten the ends of the main frame tubes—as before but at 90° to the first flattenings—and drill some holes for bolts. Don't bolt just yet, as more tubes attach at these points.

FLATTENING THE ENDS OF THE TUBE

The easiest method is to put a block of hard scrap wood on the ground, put the end of the tube over it, and knock it flat with a hammer. This can make a mess, so practice first. If you can, ask a friend to hold the other end of the tube and position a second piece of wood between the tube and the hammer. This will soften the blows but gives a good finish. For the best finish, use a big metalwork vise to squash the ends; use pieces of plywood between the vise and the tube.

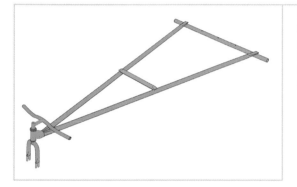

04 Now make a tube for the middle area of the frame. This is the piece that the bottom of the mast attaches to. Bolt it in position.

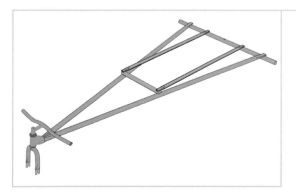

05 Use the thinner tube to make seat supports. Bolt the front ends but leave the back ends for now, as more pieces join on there.

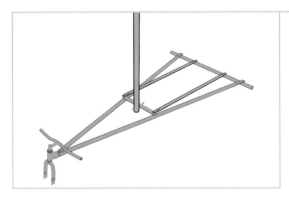

06 Attaching the mast is difficult unless you can get someone to hold it up for you. It is at this point that you probably need to take your project outside! Pre-drill the holes in the frame and the mast, locate the holes, and bolt up. Here we have used washers to increase the strength of the joint. If you let go of the mast it will fall down, so carefully lower it to the ground. Don't try to tie or prop it upright as there is no need. You may need to take the mast down for transport later on, so do not use a permanent fixing.

07 While the mast is laying flat, drill a hole 660 mm (26 ⅖ in) up for fixing the four mast struts. Make the back struts first. These determine how upright or otherwise the mast is. Assuming, after fitting wheels, that the main frame is horizontal, the cart looks better if the mast is vertical or slightly angled backward. Ask someone to hold the mast upright while you measure the distance between the fixing points. Make the back struts to correspond, bolt them in position at the back, and insert a bolt through the joint in the mast, all the while holding it in place. Make and fit the front struts, taking great care not to let go of the mast until the bolts are tight.

08 Make and fit the frame that supports the back of the seat and forms the traveler rail. A pulley will slide back and forth on this rail. This frame uses the thinnest section tube.

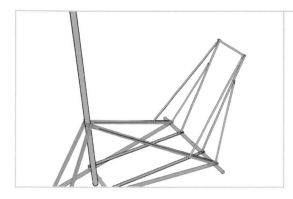

09 Now follow up with the triangulating struts. These stop the back frame from moving sideways or back and forth when the far end of the boom is moving in the wind. Some of the ends of these tubes have to be flattened and also bent to a suitable angle for fixing to the frame.

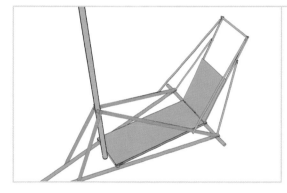

10 Measure and cut two rectangles of aluminum sheet for the seat and back. Cut with a jigsaw and metal-cutting blade—trying to use a wood-cutting blade is dangerous. As soon as you have cut the sheets, file the edges as smooth as you can. Fix the sheets with pop rivets, self-tapping screws, or small nuts and bolts. There should be no problem using rivets as there is no need to remove either sheet for transport; although, unfortunately, the sheets are difficult to paint around.

SEAT

We have used textured aluminum sheet because it is lightweight and provides good grip. Plywood is perhaps a cheaper alternative, although not quite as good-looking. Theoretically, if you want to reduce cost and weight, the seat could be half the size, but we recommend that only for experienced pilots; if your feet slip off the foot rail near the base of the mast when you are going fast, there is a chance you will injure your legs. Also, this seat is used for fixing a pulley near the mast.

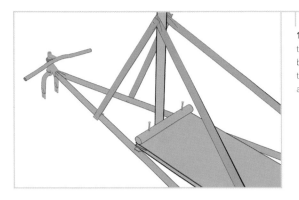

11 Make and fit a foot rail at the base of the mast. Two bolts are used; they run through the aluminum sheet and the tube beneath.

12 Make the boom bracket from steel strap (see the template on page 139). Bending the strap neatly is difficult. Make the bend gradually and evenly; hold the metal in a vise, using bits of wood either side, and gently hammer it into shape. You could, instead, look out for a similar ready-made bracket.

Mount this to the end of the boom using a nut and bolt. The bracket should rotate loosely around the mast. Drill holes in the end of the boom. Make one hole in the underside for taking a hook and a hole running through left to right for tying the sail to the boom.

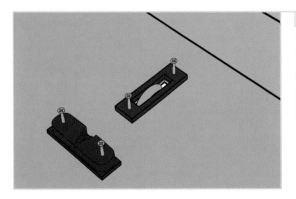

13 Fit a pulley in the seat. This channels the cord—leading to the end of the boom—from the underside of the cart to the pilot. It is a flush pulley that requires a rectangular hole sawn in the sheet and is

fixed with either short self-tapping screws or small nuts and bolts. A cleat is fitted just behind that, but its position is not critical. The cleat is used to fix the position of the cord and the boom end.

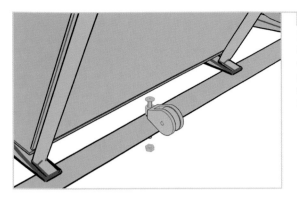

14 Bolt a pulley to the back of the cart so it is rigid and overhanging the frame. The cord from the boom wraps around this pulley and passes under the cart.

15 Now you are at a point when you can paint your cart. We sprayed it, masking the areas we wanted left unpainted. This is the quickest option. For a longer-lasting finish use brush-applied outdoor paint for metal, starting with a metal primer and finishing with a gloss paint. If you going to dismantle the cart for transport and are worried about damaging the paintwork, try a hammered paint finish.

16 Make a sail using a suitable fabric, such as canvas, strong synthetic fabric, proper sail cloth, or tarpaulin. You'll need a sewing machine and strong thread. Follow the template on page 139. Start by marking the shape with chalk and add on 10 mm (⅜ in) all around for a hem (folded-over reinforced edge). Sew the hem all around. Fold over the top and side to make tubes for the mast and boom. Pin the tube shapes and check that your mast and boom fit easily within the tube before finishing the sewing. Fix an eyelet in the corner nearest the end of the boom.

17 Clip a hook to each of the two remaining pulleys. There must be a tying point on the bottom end of the pulley—this can be part of the structure of the pulley or a proper eyelet. Clip one to the traveler rail and the other to the end of the boom. Now you are ready to thread the cord around the cart. Start by tying one end of the cord to the bottom end of the pulley on the traveler rail. Pass the cord through the pulley on the end of the boom and back down through the pulley on the traveler. Refer to the diagram for a clear demonstration.

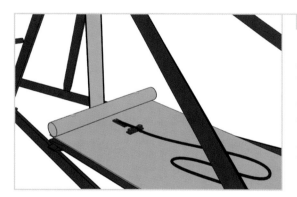

18 Pass the cord down the back of the cart behind the seat and through the pulley at the bottom of the cart. From here, travel under the cart toward the front and pass the cord up through the pulley nearest the mast. Leave the excess cord as you'll need this for letting out the boom. Finish your rigging by tying the boom to the frame near the boom bracket and tying the corner of the sail from the eyelet to the end of the boom (see diagram opposite). For the steering, drill holes in the ends of the handlebars at the front of the cart and connect to a small length of tube with cord.

PILOTING YOUR WIND-POWERED CART

An important thing to remember is that land-yachts don't use brakes; slow down by heading up into the wind and finally, when you are almost at a standstill, use your feet to stop. You must have a clear view of a safe route without anyone in the way and allow room to stop safely. Don't use it where there is any possibility of colliding with another person. If you have ever sailed a small dinghy then this cart works in a similar way. Perhaps get a few sailing lessons first.

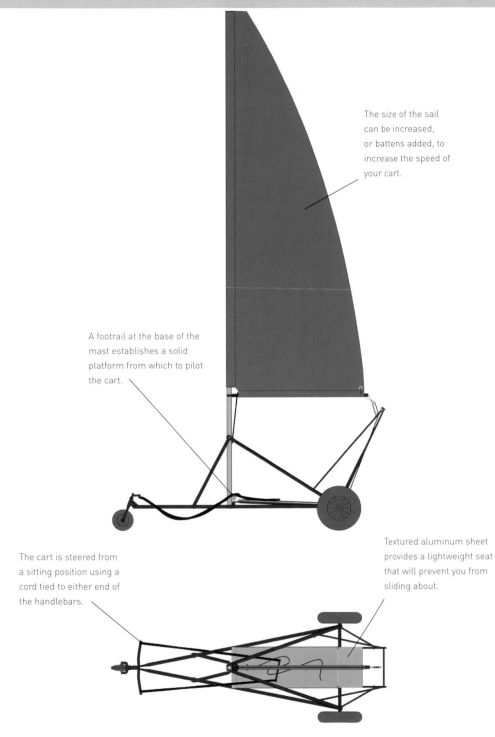

The size of the sail can be increased, or battens added, to increase the speed of your cart.

A footrail at the base of the mast establishes a solid platform from which to pilot the cart.

Textured aluminum sheet provides a lightweight seat that will prevent you from sliding about.

The cart is steered from a sitting position using a cord tied to either end of the handlebars.

6
Care, Repair, and Safety

Safety First

TAKE CARE WHEN YOU ARE BUILDING YOUR CART
AND TAKE CARE WHEN YOU ARE DRIVING IT.
You may find the safety notes the least interesting
part of this book, but it is essential nonetheless
that you prepare appropriately and take the correct
precautions.

MAKING CARTS

- When you are working with wood and creating dust you need to wear a dust mask to avoid breathing it in
- Handtools are relatively safe but should nonetheless be used with care
- Power tools are very dangerous; if you do not follow the manufacturer's safe operation instructions in the manual you may have a serious accident
- Eye protection must be worn
- Jigsaws are the safest saws. Cordless drill/drivers and electric sanders do not pose a great risk
- Electric planers and routers are dangerous and circular saws are extremely dangerous.

We have not used them in this book
- The same rules apply to all power tools: the piece of wood must be properly supported and preferably clamped to a bench; you must hold the tool properly; and if you have a free hand you must keep it far away from the blade, cutter, or bit
- Do not work if you have been drinking alcohol or taking medicine that makes you drowsy, and do not allow yourself to be distracted while working. Don't answer a phone, talk to someone, work with pets nearby, or work in hazardous conditions. Keep your workstation free from clutter

- Children must be supervised at all times. We do not recommend allowing children to use power tools of any kind except a cordless driver for driving in screws. Handtools are usually fine under adult supervision
- Metalworking handtools are quite safe, but the rough edges created by sawing and drilling are extremely sharp; take great care not to touch them, and file them smooth and rounded IMMEDIATELY after cutting the metal. Do not leave it for later
- Welding torches are extremely dangerous and can cause serious burns as well as damage eyesight. The operator and anyone

in the same area must wear special welding face masks to filter out the intense light. Any bare skin will be burned by the light from an electric arc welder (MIG, TIG etc), so cover up with non-flammable clothing
- We do not recommend allowing children to use welding gear
- Adults should seek training from an expert before attempting to weld
- Grinders are extremely dangerous. Do not allow children to use them and follow the manufacturer's instructions
- Avoid using wire brushes on a grinder (very hazardous)

IN THE EVENT OF A CRASH AND SERIOUS INJURY

We don't have enough space here to provide detailed advice, but everyone should be familiar with basic first-aid techniques, including life-saving procedures. You can find up-to-date guidelines online—for example, from American Red Cross (www.redcross.org)—but it would be even better to attend a first-aid course. It is also essential to carry a well-stocked first-aid kit with you, which you should know how to use, and a phone with which you can contact the emergency services.

CARTING

- Organized races are usually safe to attend
- Children should be supervised at all times and young children need close supervision
- Do not take your cart onto a highway or public footpath
- Where it is permitted to use carts in a public space, go slower and take every precaution to avoid hitting somebody
- Never cart down a steep hill
- Avoid carting near obstacles such as bollards, fences, and sharp or pointed items
- Wear helmets for racing or when using motorized carts
- Avoid carting near overhanging trees, pits, ditches, cliff edges, and steep drops
- Do not try performing stunts with your cart. They are not designed to be used with ramps and it is dangerous to try

MAINTENANCE CHECKLIST

Basic carts

Those with solid tires and no bearings are almost maintenance-free. You should check the bolts are tight and the wheels are secure each time you go out on your cart. DIY carts that are hastily put together have a tendency to fall apart at the seams, so take some tools such as a screwdriver, adjustable wrench, and pliers with you. All of the projects in this book recommend using only nylon-insert locking nuts—as opposed to normal nuts with no insert—so it is unlikely that any nuts will come undone as a result of vibration.

Soapbox racers

These require more maintenance, especially if you intend racing them. Race organizers will check your cart before the race anyway, which should highlight any problems. However, no one knows your cart better than you, so make it your responsibility to maintain it.

The steering will require regular maintenance; particularly cable steering, where the cable will stretch through normal use and require retensioning. This is easy to do if you have tension bolts fitted in line with the cables; otherwise, you need to unbolt the ends, retension the cable with pliers, and retighten the nuts.

Keep wheel bearings well-oiled. Don't use the cart if the bearings are dry or you will damage them.

Pneumatic tires will get punctured and are repaired in the same way as bike tires (see repairs opposite). As with all carts, you should check all nuts and fixings are tight before you use it.

Check the condition of the brake pad and replace it before it is too worn to work effectively.

Gasoline carts

These will require regular maintenance, especially if they are used often. Lubricate the chain and bearings frequently and never allow them to dry out.

The condition of the tires should be monitored. Replace them before they become bald and repair punctures in the same way as described for pneumatic tires (see repairs opposite). Many cart wheels are composed of two halves and you need to unbolt the halves to get to the tube.

Check the disk brakes for wear. Replace the disk or pad if they become worn excessively or damaged.

Nuts and fixings should be checked regularly to make sure they have not worked loose; this is important for the wheel nuts, engine mounting bolts, sprocket and disk brake screws (and or keyways), and steering linkage.

The engine is more difficult to maintain and we suggest you ask a mechanic to carry out the maintenance. The oil change is something you can do, perhaps once a year. Drain the old oil into a container and take it to a disposal facility, and replace it with a suitable quantity of the correct type of engine oil.

Electric carts

It is best to keep the batteries fully charged rather than using the cart on nearly flat batteries, so avoid doing that too often. Eventually you will need to buy new batteries, but this will depend on their age and usage. Batteries should last at least three years even if used frequently. The battery is exhausted when it no longer holds a charge.

Wheel bearings and chains require lubrication from time to time and the nuts and fixings should be checked in the same way as gasoline carts.

A gasoline engine can be quite difficult to maintain. You might want to call on the services of a mechanic to help with this.

REPAIRS

Puncture repair

Remove the collar holding the valve to the rim, use levers to pull out one side of the tire from the rim, find the source of the puncture, remove it from the tire and tube, sand the tube slightly, apply rubber solution, wait for it to become tacky, apply a patch firmly, and leave to dry for half an hour. Apply chalk over the repair—so it does not stick to the inside of the tire—and push back into the tire. Locate the valve and replace the collar, use the levers to replace the tire, and pump it up again. If you cannot identify the puncture, remove the wheel, remove the inner tube completely, pump it up, and hold under water. Bubbles will show you where the puncture is—check in the corresponding place on the tire as the cause of the puncture might still be there.

Replacement tires

Before a tire becomes bald, buy a replacement. You may want to remove the tube first to avoid damaging it. Some cart wheels, as explained opposite, have to be disassembled in order to remove and replace the tube and tire.

Paintwork

Small areas of damage can be touched up successfully if you have some leftover paint. If you don't, try to buy some of the same make and color. If not, you will not be able to match it. Spray finishes can be blended in and "cut back" (dissolved/polished); follow the instructions on the tin.

Refinishing is the best option for large areas of damage or tired paintwork. Lightly sand with super-fine sandpaper, remove grease, and check the cart is free from dust, oil, and grease. Apply two or more coats as directed.

Damaged parts

Replace wooden parts with new pieces or, if they are metal, consider welding/straightening them. Replace damaged fixings with new ones.

Further Information

All-American Soap Box Derby
www.aasbd.org
U.S. national racing program. World Championship finals are held each August at Derby Downs in Akron, Ohio

Cleveland Area Soap Box Derby
www.clevelandsoapboxderby.com
Regional soapbox racing website, with links to soapbox racing discussion forums

Deutsches Seifenkisten Derby e.V.
http://dskd.org
Official website of the German Soap Box Derby

German Soapbox Derby
www.seifenkisten-verband-bw.de/skbw/
Online resources for soap box racing in Germany

Greater Rochester Soap Box Derby
www.grsbd.com
Regional soap box racing website

Greater Washington D.C. Soap Box Derby
www.dcsoapboxderby.org
Regional soap box racing website

Kart racing
http://en.wikipedia.org/wiki/Kart_racing
Information from Wikipedia

Mission & District Soapbox Derby Association
www.missionsoapbox.com
Regional soap box racing website

Mission Museum
www.mission.museum.bc.ca
Fascinating history and detailed building instructions

National Derby Rallies
http://ndr.org
Youth program and links to local and regional soapbox derby pages

Red Bull Soapbox Race
www.redbullsoapboxusa.com
Non-motorized racing event challenging experienced racers and amateurs to design and build outrageous human-powered soapbox racers and compete against the clock in a downhill race. Not to be confused, however, with the youth soapbox derby!

Salem Soap Box Derby
www.salemsbd.org
Regional soap box racing website

Seifenkistenrennen
www.soap-box-derby.de
Soapbox racing in Germany

Soap Box Derby
http://en.wikipedia.org/wiki/Soap_Box_Derby
Information about soapbox derby racing from Wikipedia

Soap Box Racing
www.kidzworld.com/article/592-soap-box-racing
General information

www.kartbuilding.net
Information and free plans

Suppliers

All-American Soap Box Derby
www.soapboxracing.com
Official AASBD kits

Derby Gokit
www.soapboxes.com
Popular soapbox racer kit and event

eBay
www.ebay.com
Source for new and used items. Good for secondhand carts and cart parts

Freecycle Network
www.freecycle.org
Find your local network for free bicycles, strollers, and the like

Screwfix
www.screwfix.com
Fixings and wheels

www.castors-online.co.uk
A great resource if you are scouting for wheels

www.gokartheaven.com
Specializing in powered cart plans, kits, and parts

www.gokartsupply.com
Excellent source for motorized carts

www.technobots.co.uk
Excellent source for electric motors, controllers, wheels, and more

www.waycoolkits.com
Fantastic cart kits

Glossary

Ackermann steering
Steering geometry invented by Rudolph Ackermann (1764–1834) in 1810 for horse-drawn carriages and used in modern cars. At any angle of steering, the center point of all of the circles traced by all wheels will lie at a common point.

Aero ply
Extremely thin (e.g. 0.9 mm thick) and flexible birch plywood as was used in the manufacture of airplanes.

Aerodynamic
The property of a shape that performs well by offering less resistance as it moves through air.

Axle
The central shaft for a rotating wheel, sometimes fixed in position with a bearing inside the hole in the wheel. Alternatively, the wheel may be fixed to the axle, with bearings at the mounting points where the axle is supported.

Back-pedal brakes
Bicycle brakes in the rear wheel hub, operated by pedaling backward.

Batten
A small rectangular-section length of wood.

Bearing
Mechanical device allowing constrained rotation between two parts, minimizing friction by minimizing surface contact and using lubrication.

Billy carts
Australian utility cart on four wheels that is pulled by a goat. Also a cart used by children.

Bogie
See cart.

Boom
Tube (spar) at the bottom of a sail on a land-yacht and sailboat.

Boxcart
Cart made using a crate or any recreational non-powered cart.

Brazing
Joining process using a metal alloy, heated to melting temperature and spread between two or more close-fitting parts by capillary action.

Buggy
See cart.

Bull bars
Bars at the front of a vehicle to protect it and its passengers from damage in a collision with an animal or, in some modern designs, to reduce injury to a pedestrian in a collision.

Burr
The sharp edge left on metal after cutting or drilling.

Cable steering
Advanced version of rope steering using cable wrapped around a steering column to turn the front axle.

Cage
See roll cage.

Caliper brakes
Bicycle brakes. Two curved arms cross at a pivot above the wheel and hold the brake pads on opposite sides of the rim. The cable is connected to a brake lever that is squeezed, pulling the arms together and squeezing the brake pads against the rim.

Camber
The angle made by the vertical axis of the wheel and the vertical axis of the vehicle when viewed from the front or rear. Negative camber is when the bottom of the wheel is farther out than the top.

Cantilever brakes
Similar to caliper brakes, but these have each arm attached to a separate pivot point on one side of the seat stay or fork just below the rim.

Cart
Normally defined as a vehicle with two wheels; recreational carts generally have four wheels and are non-powered.

Cartie
See cart.

Center of gravity
The center of mass of a cart and its driver.

Chassis
Supporting framework.

Chock
Wheel wedge to stop the wheel turning.

Chopper handlebars
Bicycle handlebars that resemble extended cow horns.

Clutch
Mechanism for transmitting rotation, which can be engaged and disengaged and used on continuous running gasoline engines.

Coaster brakes
See back-pedal brakes.

Cockpit
The driver's seat area in a cart and racing cars.

Compass plane
A hand plane with a curved sole for removing shavings when shaping wood.

Compound miter saw
Electric circular benchtop saw capable of cutting a variety of angles across a length of wood.

Cordless drill/driver
A low-voltage rechargeable drill and screwdriver.

Counter bore
A larger hole centered on a smaller hole.

Countersink
Cone-shaped top fitting in a cone-shaped hole resulting in a flush fit (e.g. countersink screw).

Cow horn handlebars
See chopper handlebars.

Crank
A bent portion of an axle, offset but parallel to the axle, commonly used with pedals attached.

Derailleur gears
Bicycle gears using various size sprockets and a system to derail the chain and reengage it to change "gear."

Disk brake
A disk mounted to an axle and engaging with a clamp (caliper) that brakes by pressing pads on the disk. Friction slows the rotation.

Dowel
A round-section piece of wood, usually thin.

Down tube
The tube in a bicycle frame that links the head tube to the crank.

Dragster
One of the fastest-accelerating vehicle on Earth, with a long, thin streamlined body.

Drill bits
For drilling holes. Brad-point bits, with a center spike at the end, are used in wood, whereas high-speed steel twist bits can be used in wood and metal. These fit into a cordless drill. For holes larger than 12 mm diameter, use flat bits or forstner bits (wood only); for holes larger than 40 mm, use a hole saw (drill bit and drum-shaped saw combined). For holes larger than 80 mm, use a jigsaw.

Driver bits
Slotted or cross-head screws can be fixed with screwdrivers or with a cordless driver and driver bits. Choose a bit to match the screw head.

Drum brake
Shoes or pads press against the inner surface of a rotating drum, causing friction and braking. The drum is connected to a rotating wheel. Used for some powered carts.

Dune buggy
A fun vehicle with big tires, designed for use on sand dunes or beaches.

Elevation
A simplified drawn view of a 3D object eliminating perspective (an orthographic projection) for the purpose of conveying accurate building information. For example: front, end (side), and plan.

Ergonomics
The study and application of human needs in relation to designed objects.

Exploded view
A drawing showing components partially disassembled.

Forks
The part of a bicycle frame at the front that holds the wheel in position.

Gas welder
Oxyacetylene welding equipment for fabricating steel. Can also be used for brazing.

Go-cart
Powered cart. Although, also commonly used to describe non-powered carts.

Grinder
A power tool used for cutting and grinding metal and polishing.

Gudgeon
The back of a soapbox racer.

Hacksaw
Handsaw with a fine-toothed blade for cutting metal.

Hardboard
Low-cost, thin (4 mm) manufactured board with one smooth side and one textured side.

Head tube
The short tube at the front of the bike in which the handlebars are fitted.

Hub
The center part of a wheel.

Jigsaw
Handheld power tool used for cutting thin wood and thin metal, especially curves.

Kart
Alternative spelling of cart.

Keyway
A square slot running the length of an axle for locking the position of sprockets. The parts have a corresponding slot and are locked to the axle with a rectangular section key.

Kill switch
Toggle switch, button, or lever for switching the engine off.

Kingpin
The central pivot bolt in the front axle of a soapbox racer.

MIG welding
Metal inert gas welding for metal fabrication that uses a continuous wire feed as an electrode and an inert or semi-inert gas mixture.

Momentum
The product of an object's weight and speed.

Monocoque
A structure made by using an object's surface shape instead of a frame; from the French for single ("mono") and shell ("coque").

Nibs
The roughness on a wood surface during the finishing process caused by dust and raised wood fibers bonded by the paint or lacquer.

Nylon-insert locking nut
A nut with a nylon insert that reduces the tendency of the nut to work loose after vibration.

Pneumatic wheels
Wheels with inflatable tires.

Rim brakes
Bicycle brakes that act on the wheel rims.

Roll bar
Safety bar (see roll cage).

Roll cage
Steel-tube structure above an off-road cart to protect the driver during a crash.

Router
Power tool for milling slots and profiles in wood.

Seasoned
Wood that has been air-dried or kilned to eliminate moisture.

Self-tapping screws
Hardened steel screws for metal that cut a thread as they are inserted.

Solid wheels
Wheels with solid sides or with solid rubber in place of a tire and tube.

Spindle
The axle of a bicycle wheel.

Split axle
Wheels on stubs attached to the chassis. See axle.

Split pin
Used to fasten wheels, pedals etc. The ends are bent over during fitting.

Sprocket
A wheel with teeth that engages with a chain.

Stem
The front of a soapbox racer.

Straight axle
A continuous axle linking wheels on opposite sides of the cart. See axle.

Strut
A structural member.

Stub axle
A short axle joined via a bearing to a wheel. Fixed to a chassis or steering linkage.

TIG welding
Tungsten inert gas welding that uses a tungsten electrode, an inert or semi-inert gas mixture, and a separate filler material.

Top tube
The tube at the top of a bicycle, linking the head tube to the seat tube.

Try-square
A jig for marking 90° angles.

U bolt
U-shaped bar with threaded ends for fixing round-section steel to a structure.

Index